# All
# Good People
# Go To
# Heaven

✳

And Other Religious Lore

W0006194

# ALL
# GOOD PEOPLE
# GO TO
# HEAVEN

And Other Religious Lore

JIM DYET

HONOR **HB** BOOKS

*Inspiration and Motivation for the Seasons of Life*

COOK COMMUNICATIONS MINISTRIES
Colorado Springs, Colorado • Paris, Ontario
KINGSWAY COMMUNICATIONS LTD
Eastbourne, England

Honor® is an imprint of
Cook Communications Ministries, Colorado Springs, CO 80918
Cook Communications, Paris, Ontario
Kingsway Communications, Eastbourne, England

ALL GOOD PEOPLE GO TO HEAVEN AND OTHER RELIGIOUS
LORE
© 2006 by Jim Dyet

The Web addresses (URLs) recommended throughout this book are
solely offered as a resource to the reader. The citation of these Web
sites does not in any way imply an endorsement on the part of the
author or the publisher, nor does the author or publisher vouch for
their content for the life of this book.

Cover Design: Marks & Whetstone
Cover Photo Credit: © BigStock  Photo

First Printing, 2006
Printed in the United States of America

1 2 3 4 5 6 7 8 9 10 Printing/Year 11 10 09 08 07 06

All Scripture quotations, unless otherwise noted, are taken from the
*Holy Bible, New International Version*®. *NIV*®. Copyright © 1973, 1978,
1984 by International Bible Society. Used by permission of Zondervan.
All rights reserved. Scripture quotations marked NKJV are taken from
the New King James Version. Copyright © 1982 by Thomas Nelson,
Inc. Used by permission. All rights reserved. Italics in Scripture have
been added by the author for emphasis.

ISBN-13: 978-1-56292-825-4
ISBN-10: 1-56292-825-2
LCCN: 2006927278

*To my lifelong friend, Dr. Ralph S. Bell,*
*who shared the good news of salvation*
*with me when we were high schoolers*

# Contents

# PREFACE

Years ago, in Terre Haute, Indiana, an urban legend took root. Before long, it was the talk of the town. Much to the consternation of a local department store, a shopper reported encountering a viper in a bolt of cloth at the store. Rumor had it the material had come from India and had passed through customs undetected. Upon hearing this rumor, shoppers stayed away from the store. However, eventually truth won over rumor, and shoppers returned.

Like the urban legend that rose in Terre Haute, many beliefs about Christianity, God, and the Bible are simply misconceptions. In this book I attempt to weed out misconceptions and give truth an opportunity to take root. I hope each reader will carefully consider my responses to objections standing between skepticism and faith. Doing so may mark the beginning of a new way of looking at life. It may even mark the beginning of a new life!

—JIM DYET

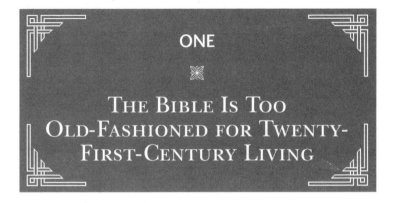

# ONE

## THE BIBLE IS TOO OLD-FASHIONED FOR TWENTY-FIRST-CENTURY LIVING

You can't go far in America without seeing a Bible. Pull out the top drawer of a dresser in most hotel rooms, and *voilà*, there it is, thanks to the Gideons International. Browse any popular bookstore and you will find a section devoted to Bibles and religion. The big-box stores carry the Bible too.

Bibles come in various shapes and sizes. Some are leather bound; others are either cloth bound or hardback or paperback. The price varies according to the binding and paper quality of the pages. The English translations vary too, from the King James Version to the easy-reading New Living Translation. If you visit an evangelical church, you may discover that most worshippers use either the King James Version or the New International Version. A smattering of other translations usually are found in church too.

You may wonder why publishers keep pumping out so many copies of such an old-fashioned book and why so many consumers buy them. Isn't the Bible too old-fashioned for twenty-first-century living?

General Motors used to run an ad for Oldsmobile insisting that its newest model was "not your father's Oldsmobile." Now the Olds is going the way of the dinosaur. The Bible, on the other hand, may not look like Dad's Bible or read exactly like Dad's Bible, but its popularity keeps increasing. It definitely will not go the way of the dinosaur.

So what makes the Bible timeless and relevant?

## The Bible's Author Knows What You and I Are Going Through

If you could write a book that provided fail-proof help for every reader's every need, wouldn't your book become a best seller? The Bible does that. It addresses the universal need for love, forgiveness, peace, a sense of purpose, and hope of eternal life. It shows how Jesus Christ meets all these basic human needs in response to faith in him.

But the Bible offers help in many other ways. It gives us comfort in times of sorrow. It encourages us when hard trials knock the props out from under us. It helps us maintain our balance in a world reeling from strife and violence. It guides us through a maze of bewildering life issues. It guards our minds against an onslaught of worries. It teaches us how to be content when inflation skyrockets. It appeals to readers of all ages.

Little children enjoy the Bible's stories. They love to retell the story of Noah and his big boat and the animals that walked on board. Inspired by the Bible's account of Noah's ark, kids often like to play with a toy ark and miniature animals or enjoy having Noah's ark décor brighten their bedrooms. Stories of other Old Testament characters such as Joseph and Moses are favorites too. Give a child a bunch of crayons and ask her to color Joseph's coat and watch her enthusiasm flow in a dazzling array of color. Kids burst with excitement when they retell the story of David and Goliath or Jesus and the feeding of the five thousand. After all, David was still a boy when he relied on the Lord to use a stone from a slingshot to drop the giant Goliath to the ground with a mighty thud. And the most important character in the story of the feeding of the five thousand, other than Jesus, is a little boy. He gave Jesus his small lunch and watched wide-eyed as Jesus turned it into a feast for at least five thousand hungry people.

Teenage readers of the Bible find that it speaks to their needs. They find guidance in the Bible for such important matters as how to have a personal relationship with God, how to get along with parents, how to respond to authority, how to relate to the opposite gender, how to select the right kind of friends, how to resist peer pressure, how to develop a healthy self-image, and how to face the future.

The Bible offers adults practical counsel too. Whether an adult is single or married, a parent or not, he can find a plethora of instructions for living joyfully and optimistically. The person who builds his life on the Bible is like a builder who constructs his house on solid rock. The storms of life will not destroy what he builds.

So why is the Bible so universally appealing and helpful? Second Timothy 3:16–17 holds the answers. This passage affirms that because God breathed out "all Scripture," it is "useful for teaching, rebuking, correcting and training in righteousness, so that the man of god may be thoroughly equipped for every good work."

"All Scripture" means nothing less than *all* Scripture. God's authorship of the Bible extends to every book of the Bible, every chapter, every paragraph, every verse, and every word. Those "begots" and "begottens" that we read in the book of Genesis are as much a part of divinely inspired Scripture as all the other words of the Bible. Books authored by men and women may be inspiring, but only the Bible is inspired—divinely inspired. As you read the Bible, you will encounter brief but powerful affirmations that God authored the Bible. Hundreds of times the Bible asserts, "Thus says the Lord"; "The Lord spoke"; "The Lord has spoken"; "The saying of the Lord"; and "The word of the Lord."

You will also read testimonials about the Bible's worth and helpfulness. Psalm 119 claims among other things that God's Word blesses, guards the heart against sinning, contains wonderful truths, fills the mind with understanding, sheds light on life's journey, is more valuable than thousands of pieces of silver and gold, is eternal, gives insight, is sweeter than honey, is true, and delivers peace to all who love it.

Jesus said that God's Word is truth and will never pass away.

The apostle Peter declared that God's Word is imperishable, living, and enduring.

The writer of the book of Hebrews described God's Word as "living and active." He declared further that it is "sharper than any double-edged sword," that "it penetrates even to dividing soul and spirit, joints and marrow," and that "it judges the thoughts and attitudes of the heart" (Heb. 4:12).

Scan the endorsements printed on the back of book jackets in your favorite bookstore. You will find some glowing endorsements, but you will not find a claim like those cited above. The Bible stands alone as a book whose origin is in heaven while its benefits extend to every area of life on earth. Because God created us human beings, he knows us thoroughly and has given us the Book we need to get to know him, obey him, and lead a fulfilling life that pleases and honors him.

## THE BIBLE'S WRITERS WERE PEOPLE LIKE YOU AND ME

God chose forty men to write the Bible over a period of about fifteen hundred years. Second Peter 1:21 tells us these writers "spoke from God as they were carried along by the Holy Spirit." These forty writers received guidance from the Holy Spirit in the selection of the words they used to write God's inspired message, the Bible. Their writings reflect different ranges of vocabulary, different literary styles, and different personalities, but their message shows an undeniable unity. (God's plan of salvation is the unified theme that ties all sixty-six books of the Bible together.) The writers did not confer with one another. Nor did they edit one another. Yet, their writings dovetailed together flawlessly to point readers to God's forgiveness through Jesus Christ.

The writers of the Bible wrote from twenty countries, employed three languages—Hebrew, Aramaic, and Greek— and represented a wide variety of occupations. Priests, judges, prophets, fishermen, poets, musicians, teachers, farmers, kings, a physician, shepherds, and government officials were among those whom God used to write his Word. Since they lived long before us they didn't drive cars, watch television, or eat at fast-food restaurants, but they were as human as we are. They made mistakes, endured trials, experienced discouragement, pondered God's ways, worked hard for a living, struggled with temptation, and experienced all the emotions common to the human race.

Moses, who wrote the first five books of the Bible, was rash, timid about speaking in public, and occasionally lost his temper. David, the sweet psalmist of Israel, committed adultery and set his mistress's husband up for murder. Jeremiah, who wrote the books of Jeremiah and Lamentations, was known as "the weeping prophet." Another prophet, Isaiah, wrote, "Woe is me." The writer of the book of Jonah possessed ethnic prejudice. Peter, who wrote two New Testament books, was impetuous—prone to "shoot from the lip." And Paul, who wrote thirteen books of the New Testament, occasionally became depressed. Nevertheless, God used these flawed men to write his flawless Word.

To their credit, the writers of the Bible admitted their flawed character and sought forgiveness. And to his credit God forgave them, but he did not expunge their record from the Bible.

Allegedly, when a portrait painter depicted Abraham Lincoln without a wart on his nose, Lincoln objected. He instructed the well-intentioned man to paint him as he was, wart and all. Similarly, God chose to show us the biblical writers "warts and all." In doing so, he revealed that the writers were quite similar to us. They were not sinless super saints, but ordinary sinners whom God forgave and used in an extraordinary way.

We can relate to the Bible more fully knowing that the writers put their sandals on the same way we do, one foot at a time.

## THE BIBLE'S PRINCIPLES ARE TIMELESS

There are timeless principles in the Bible, principles that can be used to avoid common pitfalls. The Bible includes principles for successful money management, good relationships, productive employment, wise parenting, handling hotheads, peaceful living, and much more. Many of these principles reside in the Old Testament book of Proverbs, but they are also sprinkled throughout the Bible.

Here are a few from Proverbs:

- The fear of the Lord is the beginning of knowledge. (1:7)
- Listen … to your father's instruction and do not forget your mother's teaching. (1:8)
- If sinners entice you, do not give in to them. (1:10)
- Let love and faithfulness never leave you.… Then you will win favor and a good name in the sight of God and man. (3:3–4)
- Honor the Lord with your wealth, with the firstfruits of all your crops; then your barns will be filled to overflowing, and your vats will brim over with new wine. (3:9–10)
- A little sleep, a little slumber, a little folding of the hands to rest—and poverty will come on you like a bandit and scarcity like an armed man. (6:10–11)
- A man who commits adultery lacks judgment; whoever does so destroys himself. (6:32)
- Ill-gotten treasures are of no value, but righteousness delivers from death. (10:2)
- Lazy hands make a man poor, but diligent hands bring wealth. (10:4)
- The Lord abhors dishonest scales, but accurate weights are his delight. (11:1)
- He who puts up security for another will surely suffer, but whoever refuses to strike hands in pledge is safe. (11:15)
- A generous man will prosper; he who refreshes others will himself be refreshed. (11:25)

- A prudent man keeps his knowledge to himself, but the heart of fools blurts out folly. (12:23)
- He who ignores discipline comes to poverty and shame, but whoever heeds correction is honored. (13:18)
- He who spares the rod hates his son, but he who loves him is careful to discipline him. (13:24)
- A gentle answer turns away wrath, but a harsh word stirs up anger. (15:1)
- Commit to the Lord whatever you do, and your plans will succeed. (16:3)
- Honest scales and balances are from the Lord. (16:11)
- Starting a quarrel is like breaching a dam; so drop the matter before a dispute breaks out. (17:14)
- A gossip betrays a confidence; so avoid a man who talks too much. (20:19)
- Train a child in the way he should go, and when he is old he will not turn from it. (22:6)
- A word aptly spoken is like apples of gold in settings of silver. (25:11)
- If a king judges the poor with fairness, his throne will always be secure. (29:14)
- Charm is deceptive, and beauty is fleeting; but a woman who fears the Lord is to be praised. (31:30)

## THE BIBLE'S PREDICTIONS HAVE NEVER FAILED

Long before many significant events took place, the Bible predicted them. Such predictions are called prophecies.

The Bible's prophecies foretold such significant events as the rise and fall of empires, the destruction of certain ancient cities, the fall of Jerusalem at the hands of the Babylonians, the seventy-year length of the Jews' captivity in Babylon followed by their return to their homeland, and even the name of the king who would make a decree allowing this return. However, the most significant Bible prophecies foretold the birth, life, death, resurrection, and ascension of Jesus. Most of the prophecies about Jesus were written from a thousand to five hundred years before Jesus was born. Here are several events in Jesus' life that the Bible predicted:

- ✳ He would be born in Bethlehem. (Mic. 5:2)
- ✳ He would be born of a virgin. (Isa. 7:14)
- ✳ He would bring healing and spiritual deliverance. (Isa. 61:1; Mal. 4:2)
- ✳ He would enter Jerusalem in a triumphant procession. (Zech. 9:9)
- ✳ He would be rejected. (Isa. 53:3)
- ✳ He would be betrayed. (Ps. 41:9)
- ✳ He would be mocked. (Ps. 22:7)
- ✳ He would be beaten and spat upon. (Isa. 50:6)
- ✳ His hands and feet would be pierced. (Ps. 22:16)
- ✳ He would experience excruciating thirst. (Ps. 22:15)
- ✳ He would be sacrificed for the sins of humanity. (Isa. 53:6–7)
- ✳ Soldiers would gamble for his clothing. (Ps. 22:18)

- ✸ None of his bones would be broken. (Ps. 34:20)
- ✸ He would be buried with the rich. (Isa. 53:9)
- ✸ He would rise from the dead. (Ps. 16:9–10)
- ✸ He would ascend to God's right hand. (Ps. 68:18; 110:1)

## THE BIBLE PREPARES US FOR ETERNITY

Textbooks can help to prepare a person for high school or college graduation. Some books can even help to prepare a student for exams. Certain books can help to prepare a person for marriage or the birth and parenting of a child. And a driver's manual can help to prepare a teenager for that all-important rite of passage, the obtaining of a driver's license. But only the Bible can prepare us for eternal life.

Jesus said, "The words I have spoken to you are spirit and they are life" (John 6:63). His disciples understood this. They said to him, "You have the words of eternal life" (v. 68). The Bible makes a clear, uncompromising, and irrevocable promise that all who believe in Jesus Christ receive eternal life (John 1:12). Furthermore, it categorizes all human beings as either possessing eternal life or not possessing it, and it cites only one criterion for determining which category each person fits. First John 5:12 states, "He who has the Son has life; he who does not have the Son of God does not have life." Nothing could be more defining than this truth, and nothing is more significant. Our eternal destiny hinges on whether or not we have the Son of God as our personal Savior.

## THE BIBLE IS COMPLETELY RELIABLE AND RELEVANT

The Bible has always had its critics. "There are mistakes in the Bible," they say. But no one has been able to find any mistakes in the Bible. It is not a science book, but it is scientifically accurate. For example, in Isaiah 40:22, it refers to the earth as a sphere. Centuries later, scientists caught up with the Bible's teaching about the earth, and declared that the earth is round, not flat.

Occasionally someone who has not even read the Bible charges that it is full of contradictions. Granted, a cursory reading may uncover a few apparent contradictions, but these alleged contradictions usually disappear when examined in context. For example, a critic may argue that the statement made in John 1:18 that "no one has ever seen God" contradicts Exodus 24:9–10. The latter verses report that Moses, Aaron, Nadab, Abihu, and the seventy elders of Israel saw God. However, these men saw only a form of God. In Exodus 33:20, God said, "No one may see me and live."

William Gladstone, a nineteenth-century British prime minister, claimed to have studied the Bible for seventy years. He observed, "I bank my life on the statement that I believe this Book to be the solid rock of Holy Scripture."

A century earlier George Washington commented, "It is impossible to rightly govern the world without God and the Bible."

Today, our judicial system may remove biblical references from our courts, but the Bible undergirds the very foundation of our civilization and is an integral part of our laws. If we remove Bible-based principles from our legal system, our entire civilization will fall like a house of cards in a windstorm.

Indeed, thousands of Christians today revere the Bible as God's authentic, reliable, relevant Word. The following testimonials come from people from a variety of walks of life.

> As I read and study the Scriptures, I find that there are answers to every life issue a person can come across. The answers are the same today as they were hundreds of years ago.
> —CHARLES J. BOYNTON, STAFF DEVELOPMENT
> AND EMPLOYEE RELATIONS SPECIALIST

> When confronted with everyday problems or worries, I know I can go to the Bible for comfort, advice, or just plain peace. Sometimes, I look up my particular concern in the index, and other times I just open my Bible and let the pages fall. Either way, my eyes always seem to find a story or verse that carries some encouragement and direction for my soul. While I may not always find the answer to my problem, I come away with a better perspective of the challenge ahead of me.
> —AMY SCHNIEDERJAN, ENGLISH TEACHER

> Today, we are faced with so many difficult issues. We are in dire need of stability. The Word of God is the rock I stand on when I need wisdom and discernment. I would never trust myself to make the right decision without consulting the Bible. God's Word is timeless.
> —JANET ALARIO, AUTHOR/WRITER

Reading the Bible, because it is as if God were speaking to me, gives me great peace in a tumultuous world and worrisome circumstances.

—DANIELLE GRANDINETTI, MUSIC TEACHER

The Bible helps me face the challenge of living in the twenty-first century by removing Christianity out of the realm of philosophy and into testable reality. That may seem paradoxical, as religion is thought of as an act of faith. However, the Bible makes too many claims about its origin, nature, and message to allow its followers to merely believe what it says. It is either the message from the divine Creator of the universe or it is not. Yes, it claims to be revelation from God, the supreme answer, and prophetic finale of life. Therefore, it can be compared to the records of non-Christian historians, archeologists, and scientists to determine if its claims are true. This is a rational, intellectual process that will allow judgment to be made; one can accept it or reject it. It is not just another attempt for mankind to make sense of the stars in the sky like Buddhism, Islam, and Hinduism. It can be placed in the fires of investigation by the skeptic or the critic to make it prove itself.

Having put the Bible to the reliability test, the next step is to determine if the Scriptures are useful in determining the purpose of life, your own life. Are the Scriptures relevant today? Specifically, do they give me any personal guidance in my life? Can I tap into the wisdom of the ages when making decisions or interpreting problems? Can it keep up with life as we live it this minute?

# The Bible Is Too Old-Fashioned for Twenty-First-Century Living

I am a physician, having gone to medical school after earning a master of science in anatomy. I have done a modest amount of research, published several papers in scientific journals, and received a research award during my surgical residency. My scientific work is not vast or even that impressive, however, it required enough analytical thought that an outsider would conclude that at least, I understand logic and the scientific method.

So what? I am in the position to advise you to put your mind to work and give the Bible your most thorough intellectual examination. When you look at the Bible, you will not be asked to check your brain at the door. Christianity actually requires reason and logic. If Christianity does not stand up to your analytical tests, then is it not worth believing. If it does, it will be satisfying intellectually to have proof of what you believe about the Bible.

First, look at the evidence that the Bible we have today is in fact an accurate copy of the original manuscripts. If it is inaccurate or missing major ideas or significant portions of the original message, then it cannot be trusted. Next, look at the evidence in nature to see if the biblical view of science is true. If the Bible is not accurate scientifically, it cannot be trusted to speak about science. Next, look at evidence in archeology, secular, (nonbiblical) history, and literature. The Bible should be accurate in these areas as well. I have studied these in a book called *Evidence That Demands a Verdict* [by Josh McDowell, Thomas Nelson Publishers, 1990] and recommend it for your use.

If you are willing to invest some time and thought into the Bible, it will not disappoint you. In fact, it will be more useful to you than if you accept it "by faith," without investigating its reliability. You will find the Bible to be beneficial today, in any culture, and for any person willing to test it.

—DAVID STAAB, PHYSICIAN

Principles transcend time, economies, governments, cultures, and even tax codes. Every single issue I encounter in the twenty-first century—from relationships to money management and work ethics—has an applicable principle found in the Bible.

—ANDREA BRUNZ, WRITER

As a litigation attorney, I exist in the murky and foggy world of legal interpretation and hair-splitting. Today's judicial decrees in many cases are grounded on shifting social standards, humanistic philosophies, and political pressure, which add to the instability and uncertainty of the legal process. The Bible establishes a moral compass in this uncertain world of relativity and humanism by establishing a foundation of absolute laws and moral precepts around which I can orient my thinking and my practice. The Bible also offers the hope of peace and joy to me as I operate in a world of greed, malice, and hatred.

—NORMAN E. SABIN, ATTORNEY

I use the Bible to start my day off right, to focus on the things that matter and calm my mind and spirit. During the day, I use it for entertainment. It's better than the History Channel, and there are some ripping good adventure stories. Paraphrasing the stories enhances my reputation as a storyteller with the grandchildren too.

—Lee Doffer, retired police officer

The Bible provides me with clear guidance on how to manage my priorities in a world filled with seemingly infinite choices. Basically, the Bible simplifies my life, providing me a clear path to a rich, fulfilling life in Jesus Christ.

—Bruce W. Brosch, commander, United States Navy

The Bible is my "How To ..." manual for life. It gives me a "daily dose of God," which I have found to be a better medicine for dealing with the perils of life than anything the world has to offer.

—Bill Nelson, public school teacher/administrator/coach

The Bible is indeed old-fashioned, but so are math, sunshine, smiles, families, friendships, baths, grooming, morning walks, and good meals. We should not think the Bible is outdated simply because it is old-fashioned. The Bible is as relevant for our generation as it was for all previous generations that have read it. And it will be relevant for our great-grandchildren and theirs. It will never go out of date. The apostle Peter correctly observed, "All men are like grass, and all their glory is like the flowers of the field; the grass withers and the flowers fall, but the word of the Lord stands forever" (1 Peter 1:24–25).

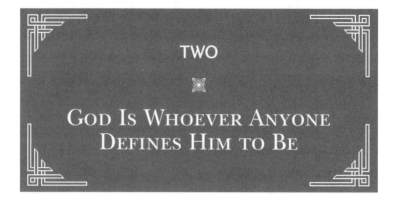

# TWO

C oncepts of God vary as widely as shoe brands and styles, and it seems we choose one the way we select a pair of shoes. If the concept suits our lifestyle and feels comfortable, we buy it. Some individuals feel most comfortable believing in an impersonal deity, one who is detached from human life. Others conceptualize a celestial Santa Claus, who sits on a puffy white cloud and eagerly responds to their every wish. For others, God is "the man upstairs" or "the big guy" or "mother nature" or "lady luck" or "the ground of all being" or "the *summum bonum*" (the supreme good from which all others are derived) or "fate" or "the force." Still others deify themselves. They worship, honor, and serve *numero uno.*

History teems with a multiplicity of gods. Ancient Egyptians worshipped numerous gods, including Ptah, artificer god at Memphis; Amun, god of Thebes; Re, the sun god; Nut, the sky goddess; Shu, Geb, and Nu, the gods of air, earth, and water; Thoth, the moon god; Mentu, the war god at

Thebes; and the nationally recognized Osiris, ruler of the hereafter and god of vegetation.

The Babylonians honored Anu, the heaven god; Bel (Baal), the king of the gods; his female consort, Ashtaroth; Ishtar, the goddess of love and war (ironic?); Nergal and his wife Ereshkigal oversaw the underworld, while Nergal was in charge of fevers, sickness, and plagues.

Numerous gods captured front and center stage in Norse, Roman, and Greek mythology. Many middle-school students can rattle off names like Odin, Thor, Zeus, Apollo, Aphrodite, Pluto, Venus, Mercury, Hermes, Artemis, Ares, Poseidon, Kronos, Bacchus, and Minerva. And they can tell you about Mount Olympus, the Roman pantheon, and Valhalla. Today, Hinduism pays homage to numerous gods, as does animism. To the animist, spirit beings reside in such things as wind, trees, rivers, fields, and mountains. Often, idols of wood and stone represent these gods.

Of course, we well-educated, sophisticated, upwardly mobile westerners would never worship idols. Or would we? Have we elevated money, fame, pleasure, gadgets, athletes, movie stars, music entertainers, recreation, success, homes, cars, hobbies, and even a slim, youthful body to the level of godhood?

Just who is God? Is he whoever anyone defines him to be? Or does he define himself in the Bible? Believing that the true God has revealed himself in the Bible, I choose to let the Bible, not human speculation, define him. Psalm

118:8, the middle verse of the Bible, applauds this choice: "It is better to take refuge in the Lord than to trust in man."

How does the Bible define God?

## GOD IS THE CREATOR

We don't have to read far in the Bible until we begin to find the answer. The first verse in the Bible affirms, "In the beginning God created the heavens and the earth" (Gen. 1:1). This brief statement answers in a few words what many scientists in the space industry have been spending billions of dollars trying to find out. How did the universe originate?

God spoke everything into existence. Skeptics might argue the point, but they cannot disprove it. Granted, our finite minds can't wrap themselves around such a vastly profound concept as creation by divine fiat, but our limited understanding does not alter the fact that God created everything from nothing. Perhaps, this penchant for explanations gave birth to the evolutionary hypothesis. Many of us would rather believe that everything evolved from a simpler form of life than believe it all came from nothing (*ex nihilo*).

But whether we attribute everything animate and inanimate to God's creative act or to an evolutionary process, we must exercise faith. Evolutionists exercise faith in their views when they present them as facts instead of theories. They cannot prove that millions and billions of years ago certain species evolved. The scientific method that calls for observation, experimentation, and verification does not apply to conclusions drawn about the evolutionary process. Can evolutionists verify their claim that certain fish became land animals? What scientific documentation from that alleged period can evolutionists cite? And when push comes to shove, evolutionists are unable to explain where the first form of matter came from. Did it always exist? If so, why is it easier to believe in the eternal existence of primordial matter than in the eternal existence of God?

At least the Bible tells the truth. It admits that "by faith we understand that the universe was formed at God's command, so that what is seen was not made out of what was visible" (Heb. 11:3). We cannot prove that God created the heavens and the earth. Neither can any theologian or scientist. By faith we accept the Genesis account of creation as true and reliable. Of course, our faith is supported by the fact that the Bible has withstood the test of time, the attacks of critics, and the investigations of skeptics. Furthermore, the Bible's predictive statements about the birth, life, death, and resurrection of Jesus came to pass without error, as have its predictive statements about other individuals, cities, and nations. So Christians stand on solid ground when they exercise faith in the Genesis account of creation.

I consider myself fortunate. I have lived in three beautiful countries: Scotland, Canada, and the United States, and I have visited forty-seven U.S. states. From the heather of Scotland, to the woodlands of Canada, to the purple mountains of the United States, I have seen God's creative power displayed.

From my neighborhood in Colorado Springs, I can view Pike's Peak, a majestic, 14,110-foot tribute to God's creative power. But you don't have to view Pike's Peak to view God's creative power. You can see it all around you—and above you.

Daily the sun rises and sets, and if you gain just a peek at it, you see God's powerful handiwork. Compared with the sun, the earth is similar to a golf ball compared with a nine-foot-diameter globe. The sun's diameter spans about ninety-three million miles. Yet, the sun is quite small compared with numerous other stars. Astronomers theorize that stars can be anywhere between a hundred to a thousand times more massive than our sun.

And many planets lie beyond our solar system. Using the orbiting Spitzer Space Telescope in 2005, astrophysicists at NASA's Goddard Space Flight Center measured light from a planet outside our solar system. They reported that the planet circles the star HD 209458 in the constellation Pegasus. This distant constellation exists 153 light years away (900 trillion miles from Earth). The newest space telescope has also detected faint light from at least 152 planets outside our solar system. David Charbonneau of the Harvard-Smithsonian Center for Astrophysics commented, "It's an awesome experience to realize we are seeing the glow of distant worlds. We've been hunting for this light for almost ten years, ever since the first extrasolar planets were discovered."

These astrophysicists are simply discovering something that resulted from the Creator's command, "Let there be light" (Gen. 1:3). How unfathomable is God's power! No wonder the psalmist wrote: "When I consider your heavens, the work of your fingers, the moon and the stars, which you have set in place, what is man that you are mindful of him, the son of man that you care for him?" (Ps. 8:3–4).

But creation teaches us more about God than the fact that he is all-powerful. He displays his infinite wisdom and orderliness in nature. From the beauty of a rose to the nesting habits of a wren, from the ways of bees to the waves of the ocean, and from the radar sense of bats to the recycling of moisture, God has shown his wisdom and orderliness. Psalm 19:1 tells us, "The heavens declare the glory of God; the skies proclaim the work of his hands." In Psalm 8:1 David exclaims, "O Lord, our Lord, how majestic is your name in all the earth!" He also credits God with putting everything under the dominion of mankind (v. 6), and credits God with the marvelous creation of "flocks and herds, and the beasts of the field, the birds of the air, and the fish of the sea, all that swim the paths of the seas" (vv. 7–8).

The human body, too, attests to God's creative genius. Our complex organs, tissues, and nerves function by design, not by accident, causing the psalmist to exclaim, "For you created my inmost being; you knit me together in my mother's womb. I praise you because I am fearfully and wonderfully made; your works are wonderful, I know that full well" (Ps. 139:13–14).

A brain surgeon told me he requests permission of his patients to pray with them before they enter the operating room. He explains that the brain is so complex that ultimately only God who designed it can heal it. "I can only do my best," the surgeon admits. "The rest is up to God."

## GOD PROVIDES FOR AND SUSTAINS HIS CREATION

We can also learn from creation that God is benevolent. After taking Noah and his family safely through the flood to a "new" world, he promised, "As long as the earth endures, seedtime and harvest, cold and heat, summer and winter, day and night will never cease" (Gen. 8:22). When we shovel snow, change a furnace filter, install air conditioning, or roll out a lawn mower, we can reflect the faithful promise God made to Noah. And when we see a farmer plowing or harvesters gathering crops or grocers stocking shelves or shoppers strolling from stand to stand in a farmers' market, we can remind ourselves that God graciously and benevolently provides for mankind. Without his providential care. John Deere and International Harvester would go out of business, the neighborhood grocery store would shut down, and consumers would starve to death.

Psalm 65:9–13 vividly expresses God's providential goodness:

> You care for the land and water it; you enrich it abundantly. The streams of God are filled with water to provide the people with grain, for so you have ordained it. You drench its furrows and level its ridges; you soften it with showers and bless its crops. You crown the year with your bounty, and your carts overflow with abundance. The grasslands of the desert overflow; the hills

> are clothed with gladness. The meadows are covered with
> flocks and the valleys are mantled with grain; they shout for joy
> and sing.

When the apostle Paul gained an opportunity to address philosophers and governing officials at the Aeropagus in Athens, he observed that they were too rigid in the devotion they paid to idols. He had wandered around their city while waiting for his friends Silas and Timothy, and had observed idols almost everywhere. The Athenians had even erected an idol "to an Unknown God" (Acts 17:23). Apparently, honoring an unknown God in this way was like taking out an insurance policy. The Athenians didn't want to jeopardize whatever good things they had going by ignoring a god they hadn't included in their plethora of idols. Paul used his moment at the Aeropagus as an opportunity to tell his audience about the Unknown God.

He identified the Unknown God as "the God who made the world and everything in it" (v. 24). He explained that this God sustains life. "In him we live and move and have our being," he said (v. 28).

Theologians refer to what we can learn about God as "natural revelation." The first two verses of Psalm 19 certainly support the teaching that God has revealed himself in nature. This passage points out that "the heavens declare the glory of God," and "the skies proclaim the work of his hands." Verses 3 and 4 personify nature as using its voice to broadcast its message about God's glory worldwide.

The apostle Paul believed in natural revelation. He wrote in Romans 1:20, "For since the creation of the world God's invisible qualities—his eternal power and divine nature—have been clearly seen, being understood from what has been made, so that men are without excuse."

But nature presents neither a foolproof picture of God nor a complete picture of him, because nature lies under the curse God imposed on it when sin entered the world through Adam and Eve. If we gauged our understanding of God's character by natural disasters and plagues, we might think he is capricious or vindictive. So we need a more complete revelation. Happily, we have it. The Bible gives us the accurate and complete picture.

Here are several facts the Bible presents about God that we could not learn from nature alone.

## GOD IS ETERNAL

In the Ten Commandments, God commanded the Israelites not to worship false gods and idols (Ex. 20:3–4). They were to worship only him. Nevertheless, the Israelites quickly broke this commandment by fashioning a golden calf and declaring it their god. It may have resembled the Egyptians' bull god Apis, but one thing is certain, the Israelites had quickly forgotten how corrupt Egypt's idolatry was. The exodus had demonstrated the true God's power over all the false gods of Egypt, but the Israelites' memory system had failed them.

GOD IS WHOEVER ANYONE DEFINES HIM TO BE

The Israelites regained their memory, but it didn't last long. Then, they regained it again and again, only to lose it again and again. Their Old Testament history is one of idolatry, regret, repentance, revival, and relapse into idolatry. Repeatedly, the Lord warned Israel that her idolatry would lead to defeat at the hands of her enemies. The culmination came in the form of the Babylonian captivity. For seventy years the Jews languished as slaves in Babylon.

Idols, then and now, are simply the works of human craftsmanship and/or imagination. They are lifeless, powerless, and dependent upon us for their existence. As we have seen, the true God is all-powerful. He is also the giver of life, and he is eternal. In Deuteronomy 33:27 God assured Israel, "The eternal God is your refuge, and underneath are the everlasting arms."

If you are like me, you wonder how the years pass by so quickly, and you begin to grasp the biblical truth that your life is "a mist that appears for a little while and then vanishes" (James 4:14). How mind-boggling, therefore, to try to grasp the unfathomable dimension of eternity and to appreciate fully God's eternal existence. But let me try.

Picture Interstate 80, stretching all the way from New York City to San Francisco, a distance of about three thousand miles. Now, picture one dime-size dot on that highway. If the dot represented the combined total number of years lived by all human beings from Adam and Eve to the present, and all the other space on the interstate highway in both directions represented eternity, the comparison would only begin to show the magnitude of eternity.

Teenagers may overuse the word *awesome*, but it appropriately describes the eternal God. He is awesome!

## GOD IS TRIUNE

Having wrestled with the fact of God's eternal existence, we can move on to another wrestling match. The challenge this time is to try to grasp the fact that God exists eternally as the Trinity. He is one God but three persons: Father, Son, and Holy Spirit. Because each person shares the divine nature and attributes equally, we say they are coequal, coessential (sharing the same essence), and coeternal.

Although the word *trinity* doesn't appear in the Bible, the concept does. First Corinthians 8:6 calls the Father "God." Hebrews 1:8 calls the Son, Jesus Christ, "God." And Acts 5:3–4 calls the Holy Spirit "God."

We glimpse a unified ministry of the Trinity at Jesus' baptism. Jesus, the Son, was baptized; the Holy Spirit descended on him; and the Father voiced his approval (Matt. 3:16–17).

After his resurrection, Jesus commissioned his disciples to proclaim the gospel worldwide, and commanded them to baptize those who believed "in the name of the Father and of the Son and of the Holy Spirit" (28:19).

Further, the apostle Paul pronounced a Trinitarian benediction at the close of 2 Corinthians. He wrote: "May the grace of the Lord Jesus Christ, and the love of God, and the fellowship of the Holy Spirit be with you all" (13:14).

No one except God can understand the Trinity, but we can accept it as a cardinal truth taught in the Bible.

## GOD IS LOVING

My wife and I were cruising the aisles of a grocery store when we met a young mother and her three-year-old daughter. The little girl was sitting in Mom's grocery cart and belting out the familiar refrain, "Jesus loves me! This I know, for the Bible tells me so." She probably didn't understand that Jesus is the second person of the Trinity, that God is all-powerful and created all things, and that he is eternal, but she knew that God loves her!

For almost seven of the nineteen years I lived in Denver, Colorado, I served a congregation as its interim pastor. During those seven years, a group of us from the church would hold a worship service every fourth Saturday at the Denver Rescue Mission. Usually, we would ask the men and women gathered for the service if they would like to request a hymn. Invariably, someone would request "Jesus Loves Me." No matter how far those men and women had wandered from home and mainstream society, they recalled that Jesus loved them.

~39~

God's love is as inexplicable as his triune nature, but it is a comforting truth taught throughout Scripture. Perhaps John 3:16 spotlights this amazing love most brilliantly: "For

God so loved the world that he gave his one and only Son, that whoever believes in him shall not perish but have eternal life."

Several years ago, a guy with a huge rainbow-hair wig—or was it his own hair?—popped up at major sporting events and displayed a prominent sign when the TV cameras zoomed in on him. The sign read "John 3:16." I don't know how this fellow managed to get one of the best seats, but he did. For example, at World Series games, his seat was right behind home plate.

My son, who is an avid sports fan, used to tell me jokingly that he would like to be a missionary to the sports world. He said if enough Christians would sponsor him, he would gladly sit behind home plate at World Series games and hold up a John 3:16 sign.

I can only wonder whether the young man with the rainbow hair attracted TV viewers to John 3:16's message or distracted them from it.

If you focus on John 3:16, you may be astounded by its message. God's love is so deep that he gave his Son for us. It is so encompassing that it embraces the whole world. It is so personal that it invites everyone and anyone to believe in Jesus. And it is so powerful that whoever believes in him receives eternal life.

~ 40 ~

Every Valentine's Day thousands of greeting cards go through the Loveland, Colorado, post office. Many volunteers stamp each envelope, "From Loveland." You can imagine the delight recipients feel upon getting a Valentine card from Loveland. But John 3:16 conveys God's personal greeting of incomparable and unprecedented love sent all the way from heaven.

## GOD IS MERCIFUL

The message of John 3:16 takes on profound significance when we place it alongside the message of Romans 3:23: "For all have sinned and fall short of the glory of God." In spite of our sins, God offers us eternal life through faith in Jesus Christ. He is indeed merciful.

But each of us must own up to our sinfulness and acknowledge our need of God's mercy. If we try to cover our sin with a pile of good works, we will not receive mercy; but if we point to a heart that needs God's cleansing, we will receive mercy.

Jesus told a story about two men who went to the temple to pray. One was a self-satisfied, arrogant Pharisee (a religious leader). The other was a tax collector, a person who exacted heavy taxes from the Jews on behalf of the Roman government and pocketed a big chunk of change for himself. The Pharisee prayed, thanking God that he was not like other men. He boasted about his fastidious fasting and tithing. The tax collector could only uncover his guilty heart and plead, "God, have mercy on me, a sinner" (Luke 18:13). Jesus said that the penitent tax collector returned home forgiven and reconciled with God (v. 14).

## GOD IS AVAILABLE

Help seems to be hard to find these days. Try finding a salesperson in a big-box store when you can't locate an item. Try to reach a doctor directly when you need one. Try to talk to a real health insurance representative by phone. Try to summon the restaurant server who told you, "Hi! My name is Jonathan. Call me if you need anything." Try to catch the attention of a check-out clerk who is locked in frivolous conversation with another check-out clerk. You've been there and done that, haven't you? Help is as elusive as Big Foot! But God is available any time to forgive sins and to grant eternal life. Romans 10:13 promises, "Everyone who calls on the name of the Lord will be saved."

*Ne Plus Ultra,* "No More Beyond," was inscribed on Spain's coat of arms until Christopher Columbus discovered America. That historic discovery showed the world there was more beyond the western horizon than Spain had envisioned. So the inscription changed, Spain's coat of arms dropped the *Ne,* leaving *Plus Ultra,* "More Beyond." This chapter has only scratched the surface of the subject of God. There is more beyond. The farther you travel in your reading of the Bible, the more you will discover about him.

# THREE

## All Good People Go to Heaven

There are a lot of good people in the world. We realize this fact when we learn of people digging down in their pockets to send aid to tsunami victims. We see human goodness in the efforts of those who risk their own lives to reach possible survivors of earthquakes, tornadoes, floods, fires, and mudslides. Human goodness resides in the hearts of loving caregivers. It clothes and feeds the homeless and others in need. It translates into numerous hours of volunteerism. The hands of compassionate doctors and nurses communicate goodness. Good Samaritans who assist stranded motorists or rescue lost hikers and mountain climbers portray goodness. The list could continue. Human goodness abounds.

It is only natural to assume that all good people go to heaven. What better reward could there be? Even many ministers, priests, and rabbis perpetuate the belief that God accepts good deeds as a kind of toll that lets people pass through "the pearly gates."

S&H Green Stamps and other value stamps were popular when I was in my teens and twenties. Merchants gave customers stamp booklets in which they could stick whatever stamps they received with each purchase. Merchandise catalogs pictured merchandise and cited the number of stamps required to purchase each item. Redemption stores carried the items and welcomed smiling customers who were ready to trade in their stamps for a toaster, a pair of binoculars, or some other item.

In those days, when a customer purchased gas for the car, a service station attendant pumped the gas, checked the oil and radiator, and washed the windshield. Some especially service-minded attendants even checked tire pressure. The fill-up cost was usually around three or four dollars, and the service station rewarded the purchase with trading stamps. Nearly every merchant gave some kind of stamps. My mother saved the stamps she received at the grocery store and traded a few booklets of them for the luggage I needed for travel to and from college.

However, good deeds aren't redeemable for entrance into heaven. The Bible doesn't support the popular belief that God weighs people's good deeds against their bad deeds and admits to heaven those whose good deeds outweigh the bad ones. The scales of divine justice do not work that way.

~ 44 ~

According to the Bible, people's bad deeds, called sins, separate them from God. Isaiah, the Lord's prophet, made this fact clear nearly three thousand years ago. He told Israel,

"Your iniquities have separated you from your God" (Isa. 59:2). Like an impenetrable, insurmountable wall, Israel's sins stood between the people and the God they professed to worship.

The people of Israel must have been shocked by Isaiah's announcement. After all, they were very religious. If you read the first chapter of the book of Isaiah, you will discover that they offered numerous sacrifices to the Lord. They burned incense to him. And they observed a host of holy days. But the Lord said, "When you spread out your hands in prayer, I will hide my eyes from you; even if you offer many prayers, I will not listen" (v. 15).

Like the people of Israel, many active churchgoers must think they are piling up brownie points with God by attending church, praying, and dropping money in the offering plate. But a million religious deeds cannot break down the wall that sin has erected between them and God.

If we were perfect, we could bypass the cross and march right into heaven, but we are imperfect. We have all disobeyed God and are therefore imperfect and unqualified to live with a perfect God in heaven. The cross delivered a powerful message from God about our imperfections—our sins—and the extent to which God was willing to go to rescue us from them.

Growing up near Niagara Falls, I made frequent trips to the edge of the Horseshoe Falls on the Canadian side of the Niagara River. Peering down through the mist, a person can see cascading, churning, swirling whirlpools. No one in his right mind would jump into such raging water, although a few souls have jumped in—not for a swim but to end their lives. The falls are unrelenting in their fury.

Picture the following fictitious scene at Niagara Falls. A daredevil anchors a long chain to a railing at a point overlooking the falls. He grabs the end of the chain and swings wildly over the churning rapids below. How many links will have to break before "Tarzan of the Falls" becomes a victim? Only one! Similarly, if I had committed only one sin (about a zillion less than the actual number), I would have sealed an eternal fate of separation from God. I would have perished because God is too holy to coexist eternally with any sinner, whether that person has committed one sin or a million sins. In the New Testament we read: "For whoever keeps the whole law [all God's commandments] and yet stumbles at just one point is guilty of breaking all of it" (James 2:10). And we know that God will not condone lawlessness and cannot coexist with lawbreakers.

Those who work in the computer chip industry know how sterile its production lab must be. Before entering it, technicians are required to shower and put on sanitized suits that cover the entire body. Otherwise, a speck of dust might contaminate the lab. If a computer chip company takes such precautions, how much more care does a holy God take to keep contaminants from defiling heaven?

Here's another analogy that helps portray the inappropriateness of even one sin in God's perfect heaven. Imagine someone offering you a glass of pure mountain spring water on a hot summer day. You can hardly wait to drink it. But what happens to your eager anticipation if the person offering the glass of water introduces a single drop of ink into the water. Now, the picture changes, and you decline the offer. Just as one drop of ink contaminates the water, so one sin would contaminate heaven. Therefore, God does not permit anyone with any unforgiven sin to share eternity with him.

A few years ago, I was invited to speak at a country club and play golf with three of the club's board members. During my two-day visit, I stayed with a board member and his wife, both of whom were charming and gracious. They also believed that good living would qualify them for a life in heaven. However, they informed me that their adult son had become a Christian and that he insisted they would not go to heaven unless they accepted Christ as their Savior. They asked my opinion.

"I agree with your son," I assured the couple. "The Bible tells us that we are saved by grace, not works. Jesus clearly taught that no one comes to the Father except by him."

To further clarify the fact that "good" people do not go to heaven because of their goodness, I invited my host to answer a golf-related question. "Jack, if God played golf, what do you think his score would be for eighteen holes?"

Jack remained silent.

"Would you agree that he would score a hole in one on every hole?"

Jack nodded his agreement.

"Then his score would be eighteen."

Jack nodded again. "I guess you're right."

"Now, Jack, you are a good golfer. You score in the low eighties every time out, whereas the average golfer never breaks a hundred. If you compare yourself with those golfers, you look really good. But if you compare yourself with God, who shoots eighteen every time, how do you look?"

Jack stroked his chin. "Not very good."

I leaned forward. "In life, we may look good if we compare ourselves with others, especially those who cheat, lie, steal, and commit adultery, but we don't look so great when we compare ourselves with God. The Bible tells us that we all fall short of his perfect righteousness. The only way we can measure up to God's standard of righteousness is to receive his Son as our Savior. The Bible also says that when we receive his Son as our Savior, God wipes the slate of our sin clean and credits us with his Son's perfect righteousness."

Because my hometown is only a couple of miles from Lake Ontario to the north and about ten miles from Lake Erie to the south, residents have ample opportunity in the summertime to visit sandy beaches and swim to their hearts' content (such opportunities are frozen in the winter). However, I did not learn to swim, because I spent my summers on a golf course.

~ 48 ~

Let's suppose an excellent swimmer from my hometown contacted me and challenged me to swim with him from San

## ALL GOOD PEOPLE GO TO HEAVEN

Francisco to Hawaii. I would have to be out of my mind to agree, but suppose I did agree, and the two of us jumped into the Pacific Ocean at San Francisco intent on swimming to Hawaii. I know I would immediately reach Davy Jones's Locker (that is, the bottom of the sea), not Honolulu. But would the strong swimmer eventually reach Hawaii, or would he end up in Davy Jones's Locker with me? You know the answer. Not even a world-class long-distance swimmer can swim that far. Similarly not even the most self-righteous, respectable citizen can reach heaven by his own efforts. The distance between a holy God and every sinner, regardless of behavior or reputation, is too vast. Only God can span the distance and qualify sinners for eternal life in heaven.

Although my parents did not attend church until I was an adult, they led respectable lives. Those who knew them well considered them good people. I did too. Dad worked hard as a door-to-door bread salesman six days a week. His day started around six with a hearty breakfast that Mom prepared. Around seven, he loaded his wagon with bread, cakes, pies, donuts, and an assortment of pastries. After harnessing a horse and hitching it to the wagon, he began his route by serving his first customer by seven forty-five. He usually arrived home by six after serving nearly three hundred customers. Mom would always prepare a delicious hot meal to welcome him.

Sundays were quiet days. Mom and Dad would read, sip tea, and listen to the radio. They regarded Sunday as the Sabbath and honored the day by resting and by sending me to Sunday school, which I attended until I turned twelve. Then I quit for two reasons: My parents didn't attend Sunday school or church, and I detested Sunday school.

I suppose my parents chose to send me to Sunday school at Knox Presbyterian Church because they and I were born in Scotland, and Scots and Presbyterians are "joined at the hip." John Knox, as you may know, was a Scottish reformer in the seventeenth century who prayed feverishly, "Gie [Give] me Scotland, or I die."

In those days, this particular Presbyterian church generally attracted upper-middle-class families, but I was a kid from a low-income home whose parents didn't belong to the church. Often, I wore cheap rubber boots (called Wellingtons) and inexpensive clothes to Sunday school, whereas the other kids wore fine shoes and expensive clothes. As a result, the rich kids made fun of me, especially when my Scottish brogue was still rolling off my tongue. I was constantly made aware that I was different.

Usually, after Sunday school I got into a fight.

Attending Sunday school for all those years may have contributed to my street smarts, but it did nothing for my knowledge of the Bible. I never learned that Jesus Christ had come to earth to die on the cross for my sin. The constant teaching was, "Be good. Obey God's commandments."

When I turned my back on Sunday school, vowing never to return, I had a vague and twisted knowledge of two Bible stories: Adam and Eve and the Prodigal Son.

## All Good People Go to Heaven

The first story went like this. The first man and woman on earth, Adam and Eve, lived in a beautiful garden, but one day they ate a rotten apple, and God kicked them out.

The second story went like this. A teenager got tired of living at home. He asked his father for some money because he had decided to leave home and live on his own. After receiving the money he asked for, he went to a big city, got involved with a bad crowd, spent all his money on booze, lost his friends, and ended up in a pigpen.

I don't think I was a poor learner or had poor Sunday school teachers, but I certainly didn't gain a Bible education. My knowledge of Scripture was practically nil, and I wrongly supposed I could earn my way to heaven by committing more good deeds than bad deeds. Whether they knew about it or not, my parents said nothing to contradict that supposition.

From age twelve to sixteen I had no exposure to religious teaching. But my life became spiritually revolutionized when I was sixteen and in my third year of high school. The remarkable change occurred because a friend persistently invited me to Saturday-night Youth for Christ rallies.

I had known Ralph Bell, who ultimately became a member of the Billy Graham Evangelistic Association, since second grade. Our close friendship continued through grade school and into high school. In our third year of high school, Ralph became a Christian, and his life advertised the fact. Everyone who knew Ralph could see quite a change in his attitudes, words, and actions, but few understood the cause. I certainly didn't until Ralph told me that Jesus Christ had changed him.

At first, when Ralph invited me to attend a Youth for Christ rally, I declined. I was so ignorant about spiritual matters that I thought only Roman Catholics spoke of Christ, whereas Protestants spoke of Jesus. I didn't know what I was exactly, but I knew I wasn't Catholic, so I refused to have anything to do with Youth for Christ. In all honesty, I probably would have declined an invitation to attend a Youth for Jesus rally anyway. I wasn't religious, and I didn't need any religious input—or so I thought. I wasn't as bad as some high schoolers, and I thought I was good enough to make it to heaven on my own someday.

However, as Ralph persisted, my will weakened. I consented to attend and gradually learned that my perceived goodness was worthless. It could not buy me a ticket to heaven. I learned that Jesus purchased admission to heaven for me by suffering for my sins on the cross. I learned further that he rose from the dead and was alive forever and was willing to save me.

One night, while attending a Youth for Christ meeting, I viewed a movie about Korean Christians fleeing communism. Often they had very little warning that communists were closing in on their villages. They used the brief moments to gather their valuables and flee. Invariably, the valuables they chose were Bibles and hymn books. I returned home, reflected on how much Jesus Christ meant to the fleeing Koreans, evaluated my priorities, and shifted Jesus Christ to the top of the list. I knelt by my bed and invited him to forgive my sins and be my Savior. I confessed that I was not and never could be good enough to go to heaven. I needed him!

After high school, Ralph Bell and I enrolled at Moody Bible Institute in Chicago to prepare for the ministry. For almost fifty years we have preached the good news that Jesus saves whoever believes in him.

The ministry has not always been easy, but it has never been boring. For instance, while I was shaking hands with worshippers one Sunday morning, a smiling, bright-eyed ten-year-old girl said to me, "Pastor, I want to ask you a question."

I smiled back. "Go right ahead."

She fidgeted a bit and then related a story. "God wanted to tell all the good people in the world that he was pleased with them. So he wrote a nice letter and handed it to an angel to deliver to all the good people."

"Interesting story," I commented.

She rocked back and forth on her heels. "Do you know what the letter said?"

"No, I don't."

"Then, you must not have been one of the good people," she laughed.

A smart ten-year-old!

I readily admit that I do not qualify as a good person who deserves God's commendation. I am simply a sinner to whom

God granted forgiveness and eternal life. Similarly, all who trust in Christ instead of in their personal goodness for salvation experience forgiveness and eternal life.

Let me share a few Bible verses with you. I think you will see at a glance that God does not forgive our sins and establish a cordial relationship with us because of our good deeds. He does so only because we believe in his Son Jesus.

> Now when a man works, his wages are not credited to him as a gift, but as an obligation. However, to the man who does not work but trusts God who justifies the wicked, his faith is credited as righteousness. (Rom. 4:4–5)
>
> For the wages of sin is death, but the gift of God is eternal life in Christ Jesus our Lord. (Rom. 6:23)
>
> For it is by grace you have been saved, through faith—and this not from yourselves, it is the gift of God—not by works, so that no one can boast. (Eph. 2:8–9)
>
> But when the kindness and love of God our Savior appeared, he saved us, not because of the righteous things we had done, but because of his mercy. He saved us through the washing of rebirth and renewal by the Holy Spirit, whom he poured out on us generously through Jesus Christ our Savior, so that, having been justified by his grace, we might become heirs having the hope of eternal life. (Titus 3:4–7)

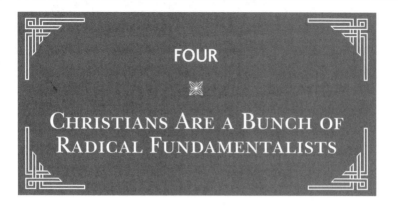

# FOUR

# CHRISTIANS ARE A BUNCH OF RADICAL FUNDAMENTALISTS

I t is nearly impossible to live in Colorado and not be a Denver Broncos fan. When the Broncos win a weekend game, places of employment buzz with joyful Monday-morning exchanges of game replays around the coffeepot or in the lunchroom. Conference room sessions get down to business only after opening remarks like, "That was quite a game yesterday," "The Broncos sure looked good," "Did you see that spectacular end-zone catch?" But when the Broncos lose, depression hangs over the state like a shroud. Employees grunt terse hellos at the coffeepot and in the lunchroom, and conference room sessions drag. Perhaps other NFL host cities experience similar bipolar emotions.

Some NFL fans are downright fanatical. The Broncos barrel man sports a hat, socks, and shoes; but his bare neck, arms, and legs protrude from a giant Orange Crush barrel that encircles his torso. Even in snow and freezing temperatures the barrel man is on hand when the Broncos play at Invesco Field at Mile High. And who can doubt the fanatical support shown to the Washington Redskins by male fans wearing dresses, frumpy hats, white gloves, and pig snouts? Nor would anyone doubt the fanatical loyalty of Oakland Raiders fans whose shoulder pads with long spikes or skulls make them look like poster boys for the Hell's Angels!

Of course, not all football fans are fanatics. I am definitely a fan, but you won't catch me wearing a barrel, a dress, or spiked shoulder pads. I suspect most NFL fans are just like me.

Just as fanaticism exists in all major sports, so fanaticism exists in all major religions. We see it in the practices of Hindu holy men who lie on beds of nails or stick long needles through their bodies. We see it in Hindu worshippers who treat rats as sacred, sheltering and feeding them in a temple, believing the rats are reincarnated ancestors. We see it in Buddhists who maintain a contemplative yoga position for many hours. We see it in animists who surround their houses with fetishes to ward off evil spirits or engage in mind-altering witch doctor–led ceremonies. We see it in suicide bombings conducted by Islamic terrorists who believe their destructive mission entitles them to eternal bliss. We also saw it in late 2004 when a Japanese man jumped into a lion exhibit and attempted to convert two lions. One bit and mauled him. No one would question his religious fanaticism—or his psychological aberration.

Christian fanatics do dumb things too, but these fanatics are few compared with the many rational and reasonable followers of Christ. Unfortunately, media attention focuses on the few fanatics and largely ignores those who go about their business in a quiet manner. I cringe as I watch TV coverage of Christians protesting a gay pride parade in a rowdy manner. Cameras zoom in on signs like, "You will burn in Hell, faggots!" "God hates homosexuals!" and "Turn or Burn!" God can get along quite nicely without that kind of representation.

Just once, it would be a breath of fresh air to see network news coverage of Christians befriending homosexual members of the community. Every day Christian doctors and nurses care for AIDS patients who contracted the disease through homosexual relations. Their dedication is surely worth an occasional segment of the nightly news!

I have yet to meet a Christian who believes homosexuality is a legitimate sexual orientation, but I have met many who refuse to single out homosexuals as objects of divine wrath. Although the Bible states that God detests homosexuality, he also detests lying, cheating, stealing, murder, hate, hypocrisy, egoism, vanity, adultery, envy, covetousness, greed, prejudice, self-centeredness, and a host of other sins. He sees all humankind as sinful and lost, but he offers forgiveness through his Son, Jesus, to all. Jesus died for all sinners, not just "straight" sinners.

First-century Corinth had a bad reputation even by pagan standards. This sin city of ancient times, where East and West embraced on the crossroads of Graeco-Roman culture, was notorious for its drunkenness and blatant immorality. A thousand prostitutes plied their trade at the temple Corinth had built to honor Aphrodite, the goddess of love. Throughout the Greek and Roman world, people used such terms as "Corinthian sickness" and "to Corinthianize" when they referred to sexual immorality. But a colony of Christians sprang to life in Corinth and became Exhibit A for the truth that Jesus Christ gives new life for old. When the apostle Paul wrote his first letter to these new Christians, he reminded them that some of them had led typical Corinthian-style lives before they believed in Christ (1 Cor. 6:9–11). Some had been sexually immoral or idolaters or adulterers or male prostitutes or homosexual offenders or greedy or drunkards or slanderers or swindlers. But God had converted these debased Corinthians into redeemed Christians.

Since God is no respecter of persons, Christians who single out a group of people for condemnation are unlike him. Jesus taught his followers to love God supremely and to love their neighbors as themselves. When an expert in Jewish law asked Jesus what he meant by "neighbor," Jesus related the story of the Good Samaritan. According to the story, a Samaritan rescued a traveling Jew who had been mugged, robbed, and left for dead. In spite of the fact that the Jews held a long-standing disdain for Samaritans, this Samaritan responded to the dying man with compassion and care. He even picked up the tab for the injured man's lodging and medical expenses. The Samaritan acted as the neighbor Jesus told the Jewish scholar to love (see Luke 10:25–27).

We as Christians should love, not lambaste; care about, not consign to hell; minister to, not malign our gay or lesbian neighbor. Jesus died for everyone, and his love extends to everyone. Christians find homosexual practices offensive, but they should not ostracize gay and lesbian "neighbors" from God's love and withhold Jesus' invitation to believe in him and find forgiveness and a new life.

Sincere Christians model their lives after the life of their Lord and Savior. In the Gospels, which portray his life, we see Jesus rubbing shoulders with the people of his day. He turned no one away who needed his teaching and healing. He always made time for the alienated, the abused, and the outcast.

While his countrymen skirted Samaria on their way from Judea to Galilee to avoid contact with the despised Samaritans, Jesus intentionally took the route that went through Samaria. At noon on one such journey, he sat by a well outside a village and engaged a Samaritan woman in conversation. Apparently, the poor woman had braved the scorching sun to draw water at noon rather than go there when the other village women ordinarily drew water. They would probably have given her a rough time because of her multiple marriages and current live-in arrangement. So there she was, ostracized by her own people, the Samaritans, and the object of disdain by the Jews. But Jesus was a different

~ 59 ~

kind of Jew. Not one grain of racial prejudice resided in him, much to the Samaritan woman's amazement. She asked him, in effect, "How come you are talking to me? After all, the Jews have nothing to do with Samaritans."

From that point, Jesus' further conversation guided her to the realization that he was the Messiah, the Savior whose arrival the Old Testament had predicted. This personal discovery prompted her to rush into her village and tell others that she had found the Messiah.

Before long a stream of Samaritans rushed to Jesus. They were so enthralled with him that they invited him to be their guest. Jesus accepted the invitation and remained in the village two days. John 4:39–42 reports that many believed in him because of the Samaritan woman's convincing testimony and because of what they learned firsthand from Jesus.

The people of Jesus' day also shunned lepers. Lepers were forbidden to enter within a town's limits, and if they saw anyone approaching, they were obligated to shout the warning, "Unclean! Unclean!" But Jesus welcomed lepers into his presence and healed them. Luke 17:11–19 reports that on one occasion ten lepers stood at a distance from Jesus. "Have pity on us," they called out.

Jesus immediately healed them. Fear and disdain had drawn a circle that shut them out, but Jesus' love drew a circle that brought them in!

In the Gospels, we see repeatedly that the religious officials exuded personal pride, hypocrisy, and prejudice, and opposed Jesus vehemently. After all, Jesus befriended the very people they hated and excluded. Luke 7:36–50 relates that they raised quite a ruckus when Jesus allowed a woman of ill repute to anoint his feet. Her tears mingled with the ointment as she acted out her devotion to Jesus. The religious leaders babbled on about how a true prophet would never allow such a sinful woman to get near him.

On a similar occasion, Jesus ate in the home of Levi, a tax collector, and with many of Levi's tax-collector buddies and others whom the religious leaders classified as sinners. Because tax collectors in Israel worked for the occupying Roman forces and often ripped off their own countrymen, the population considered them the scum of the earth. Understandably, the arrogant religious officials could not comprehend Jesus' willingness to socialize with such "riffraff." And they were quick to condemn Jesus' association with the dinner guests. But those whom they despised, Jesus loved (Luke 5:27–31).

Even when he was dying on the cross, Jesus showed a spirit of unrivaled forgiveness. In response to those who hurled insults at him, Jesus prayed for them, saying, "Father, forgive them, for they do not know what they are doing" (Luke 23:34).

When a thief pinioned on a cross beside Jesus implored Jesus to remember him in his kingdom, Jesus answered, "I tell you the truth, today you will be with me in paradise" (v. 43).

This thief had likely led a vile and violent life, but because Jesus reached out to him with love and forgiveness, he could die in peace, knowing that he would enjoy eternal life with Jesus.

Obviously, Jesus loved people, even those whose behavior shocked and alienated most of society. And he still loves such people—the outcasts and the downcasts, the renegades and the reprobates, the distanced and the debased. He does not exclude sinners or excuse their sin. He embraces sinners and emancipates them. And all who claim to follow Jesus must follow his example.

Some who threaten abortion doctors and jeer gays claim to be Christians, but in my judgment they fall far short of Jesus' example of love. In all fairness, some pro-abortionists and gays spew hatred and insults at Christians. They lump all Christians together as "fundamentalists," and equate the term with the most intolerant, narrow-minded group on the planet.

Does the term *fundamentalist* conjure up images of hateful, fanatical, wild-eyed, narrow-minded militants in your mind? Perhaps, we need to examine this term in its historical context.

Historically, the movement called "fundamentalism" grew out of a desire to preserve biblical integrity. The term was coined at the turn of the twentieth century in response to liberal theology. The liberals denied such long-held tenets as the inspiration of the Bible, the virgin birth of

Christ, Jesus' deity, the authenticity of his miracles, his sinless life, his blood atonement, his bodily resurrection, and his second coming. The liberals, known back then as "modernists," had cutting words for those who believed that Jesus shed his blood to provide salvation freely for all who those who believe in him. They accused them of promoting "a slaughterhouse religion."

By the 1920s theological modernism had blanketed major Protestant denominations, but a few biblical scholars raised their voices in defense of the fundamentals of historic faith. In a series of books called *The Fundamentals* (1909–1915), they defended the tenets that the modernists denied. Hence, those who advocated faith in historic biblical teachings became known as "fundamentalists."

The rocky era of fundamentalism/modernism controversy witnessed several partings of the ways in America's religious institutions and denominations. For instance, Gresham Machen, a Presbyterian scholar, and several other theologians withdrew from Princeton Theological Seminary. They felt strongly that religious modernism had sullied their institution's honor. Some churches, too, withdrew from modernist-controlled denominations. Some of these churches formed associations, fellowships, and new denominations. Others remained unaffiliated.

Today, millions of Christians hold to the fundamentals of historic biblical Christianity and are, therefore, fundamentalists, but they are not fanatical fundamentalists. They recognize the fact that the United States is a pluralistic nation that upholds individual rights. They are tolerant of lifestyles that contradict biblical injunctions, but they endeavor by peaceful and loving means to persuade others to abandon such lifestyles and embrace biblical faith and conduct.

Name-calling drives a wedge between those who hurl insults and the insulted, but genuine love removes the wedge and closes the gap. Jesus said his followers were to be salt and light (Matt. 5:13–16). Lighthouses do not blow horns; they merely shine. Salt creates thirst. If Christians function as salt and light, their persuasion will be incontrovertible, even if they speak softly.

C hristmas was only three weeks away when an ad in the
Colorado Springs newspaper grabbed my attention.
Citing a report in *Time* magazine, the ad claimed that 67 percent of Americans believe in angels and 46 percent "know
they have a personal guardian angel." Next, the ad invited the
public to hear lectures on angels, which would show atten-
dees how to "communicate with spiritual helpers and find life
purpose." The lectures promised to provide "practical tech-
niques to unfold your spiritual gifts of prophecy, clairvoyance,
clairaudience, and healing to become more successful in your
personal, business and social life."

When Harry Carey, the inimitable Chicago Cubs'
announcer, died in California in the spring of 1998, baseball
fans everywhere felt they had lost a close friend. It didn't matter that throughout his career Carey had mispronounced
more than a few players' names. His love of baseball and its
fans more than compensated for the mispronunciations. Who
can forget the image of Carey leaning out the broadcasting

booth at Wrigley Field and leading the assembled fans in a full-throttle rendition of "Take Me Out to the Ballgame"? Of course, another Carey trademark was stamped onto the end of every Cubs' victory when he shouted, "Cubs win. Cubs win! Holy Cow!"

The news of Carey's death sent Chicago's TV sports reporters into the streets to ask hometown Cubbies fans how they were handling the fact that Carey had passed away. One distraught young lady lamented that Wrigley Field just wouldn't be the same without Carey in the broadcast booth, but she stated that he would always belong to the Cubs. "Next season, Harry will be our angel in the outfield," she intoned.

The fan's idea that good people become angels when they die is not an isolated one. Many share her belief. I'm sure it's comforting to believe a departed loved one or dear friend is sitting on a white, puffy cloud up yonder (or over Wrigley Field), strumming a harp or waving a microphone, but is it an ill-founded belief? What does the Bible teach about angels? What does it teach about the human condition after death?

Angels are mentioned about three hundred times in the Bible, and their divinely assigned roles are significant. God created billions of angels to perform his will. Daniel 7:10 refers to angels as "thousands upon thousands" ministering to him and "ten thousand times ten thousand" standing before him. Revelation 5:11–12 mentions a throng of "many angels, numbering thousands upon thousands, and ten thousand times ten thousand" who "encircled the throne" of God, praising him. These created beings (Col. 1:16) witnessed God's creation of the universe and joyfully applauded the accomplishment (Job 38:4–7).

Unlike human beings, angels are bodiless. Psalm 104:4 (NKJV) reveals that the Lord "makes His angels spirits." However, in Bible times angels occasionally assumed a physical appearance. Two angels in human form accompanied the Lord on a visit to Abraham and ate a meal Abraham served them (Gen. 18:1–8). Two angels also appeared in human form to Abraham's nephew Lot (19:1–5).

King David correctly made a distinction between angels and human beings in Psalm 8:4–5 when he asked of God:

> What is man that you are mindful of him, the son of man that you care for him? You made him a little lower than the heavenly beings [angels] and crowned him with glory and honor.

The Bible offers only rare glimpses of the condition of deceased human beings, but none of those occasions feature them as angels. So don't expect to trade your walking shoes for wings and your hat for a halo when you enter heaven. The Bible portrays departed human beings as departed human beings.

For example, Luke 16:19–31 pulls back the curtain of eternity so we can view two deceased men. We see an unnamed man, who was rich in his lifetime, and a poor man named Lazarus. During his life on earth, Lazarus had begged at the rich man's gate. Lazarus had endured ill health, hunger, and humiliation on earth, whereas the rich man had maintained a lavish lifestyle. However, death had turned the whole picture around. The rich man experienced suffering and anguish in the afterlife, while Lazarus enjoyed consolation and comfort in paradise. The next life rights wrongs. It afflicts unbelievers who were previously comfortable, and it comforts believers who were previously afflicted. But it doesn't change anyone into an angel.

On one occasion Jesus took three disciples, Peter, James, and John, to a mountaintop. Suddenly two visitors from "the other side" appeared and talked with Jesus. Somehow, Peter and perhaps the other two disciples recognized the visitors as Moses and Elijah. Both men had exited life on earth centuries before Jesus and his disciples climbed the mountain. Obviously, Moses and Elijah looked like men, not angels.

First Samuel 28 provides an intriguing look at the deceased. The occasion was King Saul's visit to a medium, the witch of Endor. Saul had been rapidly declining politically, spiritually, and physically, and was just about at the end of his rope. His most powerful enemy, the Philistines, had gathered *en masse* to fight Saul's army, and terror was wrenching his heart. Aching for direction, he asked the medium to bring the prophet Samuel from "the other side."

Likely, the witch resorted to illusion in her attempt to deceive Saul, but it seems that Samuel actually appeared and shocked her.

"What does he look like?" [Saul] asked.

"An old man wearing a robe is coming up," she said (v. 14).

It is worth noting that she did not describe Samuel as an old angel or even a young angel. Clearly, he resembled a man!

So what happens to a person who dies?

"Dust to dust. Ashes to ashes." These words spoken at interments echo the first part of Solomon's brief commentary on death. He wrote in Ecclesiastes 12:7 that "the dust returns to the ground it came from." But is that all we can expect after gasping our last breath? No! Solomon continued, "and the spirit returns to God who gave it" (v. 7). We must look to other Scripture passages, though, to round out the picture Solomon painted with a broad brush.

Writing under house arrest as a prisoner of Rome, the apostle Paul did not know whether he would be released or executed, but he was prepared for either eventuality. Release from prison would enable him to minister on behalf of his friends, the Christians at Philippi. Execution would transfer him immediately into the presence of Christ. He referred to these two possibilities this way:

> I am torn between the two: I desire to depart and be with Christ, which is better by far; but it is more necessary for you that I remain in the body. (Phil. 1:23–24)

In his second letter to the Corinthians, Paul indicated that a believer's death separates that person from the body but unites the individual with the Lord. "We are confident," he wrote, "and would prefer to be away from the body and at home with the Lord" (2 Cor. 5:8). Identifying with Paul's perspective on death, an elderly preacher commented:

"Christianity is good when you are living, better when you are dying, and best when you are gone."

However, an unbeliever cannot look death in the eye confidently and peacefully. To the unbeliever, death is not only unpleasant and humbling, it is a horrible nightmare come true. At death the unbeliever experiences divine judgment (Heb. 9:27). An unbeliever enters hades (hell), a place of conscious suffering and separation from God (Luke 16:23).

The body will rejoin the spirit someday though. Jesus spoke about two future resurrections, a resurrection unto life and a resurrection unto condemnation (John 5:28–29). The first phase of the resurrection unto life will take place at the rapture, when Jesus will come *in the air* to catch away his church from the earth. The bodies of deceased Christians will exit graves, be transformed into glorified bodies, and rejoin their "owners" (1 Cor. 15:50–54; 1 Thess. 4:16). The second phase of the resurrection unto life will occur when Christ returns *to the earth* to establish his kingdom. The bodies of deceased Old Testament and tribulation martyrs will be raised, glorified, and reunited with their "owners" (Dan. 12:1–3).

The second resurrection, the resurrection unto condemnation, will occur at the end of Jesus' kingdom reign. The bodies of all unbelievers will be raised and united with their "owners" as a brief prelude to the great white throne judgment. God will judge this mass of faithless humanity on the basis of their individual rejection of Christ and will consign them to eternal suffering and separation from God in the lake of fire.

Revelation 20:14–15 describes this final judgment in brief but graphic detail:

> Then death and Hades were thrown into the lake of fire. The lake of fire is the second death. If anyone's name was not found written in the book of life, he was thrown into the lake of fire.

Some tombstone epitaphs give those who read them reason to reflect on the brevity of life and the certainty of death. One such epitaph advises:

> Pause, my friend, as you pass by.
> As you are now, so once was I.
> As I am now, so you will be.
> Prepare, my friend, to follow me.

Upon reading this epitaph, a visitor left a written note:

> To follow you is not my intent
> Until I know which way you went.

In the normal course of life, each of us will encounter death. It will be personal and transitional. We will pass from the body and enter eternity. None of us will become an angel, but those of us who believe in Jesus as Savior will enjoy the eternal benefits God has reserved for his sons and daughters. Angels will marvel at the love and grace that escorted us safely through earth's trials and sorrows, including death itself, and carried us to our Father's house.

# SIX

※

# THE END IS NEAR!

Cartoonists have a field day with the announcement, "The end is near!" They show a little old guy with a white beard holding up a "The end is near!" sign. Maybe the end is near for little old guys with white beards. They don't have much longer to live. But is the end near for the rest of us? Is the world about to blow up or melt down or wash away or freeze to death?

The horrific 9/11 tragedy sent people scurrying for the answer. Millions looked for the answer in the popular *Left Behind* series written by Jerry Jenkins and Tim LaHaye. The quest for answers about the end times made the two authors frequent guests on TV talk shows. For a while, after 9/11, church attendance climbed. People definitely wanted to be in God's good graces if the end was near.

Also, recent cataclysmic natural disasters have spiked curiosity about the end of the world. Many people see an end-time warning sign in every disaster, from California's mudslides to the horrific tsunami in Asia the day after

## The End Is Near!

Christmas 2004 and the large earthquake in the same area the day after Easter 2005. And the proliferation of nuclear capability among nations unfriendly to democratic countries touches off cries of "The end is near!"

Christians hold different views of the end times. After World War I, dubbed the war to end all wars, some religious leaders believed conditions on earth would get better and better—Christianized—and lead to Christ's return. According to this view, called *postmillennialism,* eternity follows Christ's return. However, World War II erupted and dashed much of this optimism.

Other Christians, refusing to see the world through rose-colored lenses, suggest that conditions will deteriorate until they reach a horrendous all-time low. This low, they say, will mark the tribulation, a seven-year period in which the devil will exercise vast powers over human life through his puppet ruler, the antichrist. According to this view, Jesus Christ will return to earth at the end of the tribulation, destroy the antichrist and his cronies and their vast following, and set up his kingdom on earth, which they say will last one thousand years (a period called the millennium). This view is known as *premillennialism.*

Another school of thought, called *amillennialism,* teaches that eternity begins when Christ returns. According to amillennialism, our planet will not experience either a tribulation or a thousand-year reign of Christ. Amillennialists believe good and evil—God's kingdom and Satan's kingdom—exist in the world and will continue to do so until Christ returns. At that time, God will raise the dead, judge all human beings, and inaugurate the eternal state.

Now, back to premillennialism.

To complicate matters, premillennialists fall mainly into three main categories: pretribulationists, midtribulationists, and posttribulationists. Another group, which holds a view quite similar to the midtribulationists' view, is the prewrath group. Pretribulationists believe that before the tribulation, Jesus will come from heaven to earth's atmosphere and catch Christians away from earth (the rapture). This is the view advanced in the *Left Behind* series. Others, midtribulationists, think Christians will experience the first half of the tribulation before being raptured. Still others, posttribulationists, teach that Christians will live on earth for all seven years of the tribulation. According to posttribulationists, the rapture will occur after the tribulation.

## VIEWS REGARDING THE RAPTURE

- ※ Pretribulational View: Jesus catches Christians away from the earth before the tribulation.
- ※ Midtribulation View: Jesus catches Christians away from the earth in the middle of the tribulation.
- ※ Posttribulation View: Jesus catches Christians away from the earth at the end of the tribulation and returns them to the earth for the thousand-year kingdom rule.

Hold on! There's more.

## The End Is Near!

A popular belief among Christians concerns signs of the times. According to this belief, major events of earth will occur as signs that the rapture is approaching quickly. "Jesus is coming soon" is a message you may have seen on a bumper sticker. I spotted these words on a Pennsylvania barn. Presented in large, red-painted letters, JESUS IS COMING SOON caught the attention of passing motorists. So did the large ad beneath it that read: CHEW MAIL POUCH TOBACCO. I wonder, is tobacco chewing recommended as a way to prepare for Jesus' coming?

This chapter presents the pretribulational view that Jesus may rapture Christians at any time and that no signs have to precede the event. The rapture may occur today, a hundred years from now, or at some other future time. We can predict the event, but we cannot predict the date.

But first we need to understand why so many Christians have picked up the notion that the rapture is close at hand because of so-called signs of the times. Their belief lies in a popular interpretation of what is often referred to as Jesus' "Olivet Discourse," found in Matthew 24–25, Mark 13:1–37, and Luke 21:5–36. But is it correct?

The Olivet Discourse followed a question Jesus' disciples asked him: "What will be the sign of your coming and of the end of the age?" (Matt. 24:3). Jesus responded by citing a number of signs that will precede his coming.

Before mentioning these signs, we ought to clarify two things: (1) Jesus was addressing Jews, those who anticipated the coming of the Messiah to establish his earthly kingdom; (2) the rapture is not Jesus' return to establish his earthly kingdom; it is an entirely different event. At the rapture Jesus will catch away Christians from the earth, but he will not set foot on the earth. At the rapture, he will take believers bodily to heaven; whereas, when he comes to the earth to establish his kingdom, he will bring a bit of heaven to the earth. As a matter of fact, his earthly kingdom is often called "the kingdom of heaven" in the Gospels. Therefore the signs Jesus predicted must happen before he comes to the earth to reign, but they do not have to happen before he comes in the air to rapture believers.

With these points in mind, consider the signs Jesus gave:

## FROM MATTHEW 24:1–29

- ※ false messiahs (vv. 4–5)
- ※ wars and rumors of wars (v. 6)
- ※ international conflict (v. 7)
- ※ famines (v. 7)
- ※ earthquakes (v. 7)
- ※ persecution and martyrdom (v. 9)
- ※ religious apostasy (v. 10)
- ※ false prophets, deceivers (v. 11)
- ※ increase of wickedness (v. 12)
- ※ gospel of the kingdom preached to all nations (v. 14)
- ※ abomination in the temple (v. 15)
- ※ counterfeit miracles (v. 24)
- ※ solar and lunar eclipses (v. 29)
- ※ falling stars and planetary distress (v. 29)

THE END IS NEAR!

## FROM MARK 13:1–37

- false messiahs (vv. 5–6)
- wars and rumors of wars (v. 7)
- international conflict (v. 8)
- famines (v. 8)
- earthquakes (v. 8)
- persecution (v. 9)
- gospel of the kingdom preached to all nations (v. 10)
- family breakdown (v. 12)
- abomination in the temple (v. 14)
- counterfeit miracles (v. 22)
- solar and lunar eclipses (v. 24)
- falling stars and planetary distress (v. 25)

## FROM LUKE 21:5–36

- false messiahs (v. 8)
- wars and revolutions (v. 9)
- international conflict (v. 10)
- earthquakes, famines, pestilences (v. 11)
- persecution of believers (vv. 12–19)
- Jerusalem surrounded by armies (v. 20)
- signs in the sun, moon, and stars (v. 25)
- roaring and tossing of the sea (tsunamis?; v. 25)
- terror and heart failure (v. 26 NKJV)
- celestial shaking (v. 26)

It is easy to see at a glance why many Christians equate current calamities and distresses with the signs Jesus predicted in the Olivet Discourse. However, many Bible teachers equate these signs with horrific events described in the book of Revelation as occurring between the rapture (Rev. 4) and Christ's coming to earth to reign (Rev. 19). This interval is the tribulation period, and the predicted events are described in Revelation 6—18.

If premillennialists are right, and I believe they are, and Jesus were to rapture Christians from the earth today, earth's future would include seven years of tribulation followed by Jesus' thousand-year reign on earth (Rev. 20:4–6).

So the earth is not going to implode, explode, or self-destruct. It will be around for a long, long, long time. As a matter of fact, two thousand years before Jesus' birth God promised Abraham, the father of Israel, that he would give him and his descendants the land of Canaan (Palestine) as "an everlasting possession" (Gen. 17:7–8). If Planet Earth were to come to an untimely end, so would Palestine. However, God pledged that the land of Palestine would exist forever.

This Promised Land, which we now call Palestine, will mark the center of Jesus' kingdom reign, and in case you are wondering what conditions on earth will be like when Jesus reigns from Palestine, let me share a brief biblical description of those conditions. I am sure you will see a striking contrast with current conditions.

- Deserts and wasteland will blossom profusely. Forests will spring up, and grasslands will cover the land. (Isa. 35:1–2, 7)
- The blind will see; the deaf will hear; the lame will leap; and the mute will shout for joy. (vv. 5–6)
- Water shortage will be a thing of the past. (v. 7)
- Gladness and joy will replace sorrow and sighing. (v. 10)
- The Dead Sea will become a freshwater fisherman's paradise. (Ezek. 47:9–10)
- Longevity and good health will prevail. (Isa. 65:20; Rev. 22:2)
- There will be no power outages. (Isa. 60:19–20)
- The infant mortality rate will be zero. (Isa. 65:20)
- Everyone will eat well and live securely. (vv. 21–22)
- Property rights will be respected. (Mic. 4:4)
- Violence will cease, and prisons will be empty. (Isa. 60:18)
- The streets will be safe for children. (Zech. 8:5)
- Children will be safe even around snakes. (Isa. 11:8)
- Wild animals will abandon their savagery. Former predators and prey will live in harmony. (vv. 6–7)
- Previously carnivorous animals will be herbivorous. (v. 7)
- Universal peace will prevail. (Isa. 9:7)
- Jesus will judge righteously, justly, and decisively. (Isa. 11:3–4)

- Israel will be exalted among the nations. (Zech. 14:16)
- Knowledge of the Lord will pervade the earth. (Isa. 11:9)
- Righteousness and holiness will be reflected in even the most unexpected places. (Zech. 14:20–21)

What a pleasant place it will be when Jesus is king over all the earth! Color codes signifying levels of terror alerts will fade into obsolescence. No one will ever face an outbreak of flu or any other epidemic. Hospices will no longer be needed. Burials will be extremely rare. We will not have to lock our doors or carry homeowners insurance. Amber alerts will be things of the past. Sex offenders will not live in Jesus' kingdom. If sports venues exist, they will be free of violence and cussing. The newspapers and TV networks will have only good news to broadcast. No one will have to worry about Social Security going bankrupt or CEOs stealing company funds or hoodwinking stockholders. Not one case like that surrounding Terri Schaivo's feeding tube will divide human opinion. We will not have to wonder how our political leaders will respond to nuclear buildups in unfriendly nations. Nor will a natural disaster occur anywhere in the world. Peace will prevail among individuals, nations, and the forces of nature.

So don't look around you and feel hopeless, thinking the world is about to end. Instead, look above you to the Lord of heaven and earth and anticipate a better day for Planet Earth.

But there is more!

## THE END IS NEAR!

After Jesus rules our planet for a thousand years, God will judge all unbelievers and consign them to the lake of fire (Rev. 20:11–15). Then he will renovate Planet Earth, ridding it of all vestiges of sin. Eternity will commence.

Here are a few verses that describe earth's brand-new day:

"Behold, I will create new heavens and a new earth." (Isa. 65:17)

I saw a new heaven and a new earth [new in quality], for the first heaven and the first earth had passed away." (Rev. 21:1)

But in keeping with his promise we are looking forward to a new heaven and a new earth [new in quality], the home of righteousness. (2 Peter 3:13)

When God created our planet, he saw everything he had made, and he pronounced it "good" (Gen. 1:31). But the human race has scarred it, exploited it, stripped it, littered it, burned it, and bombed it. Someday, God will renovate it. Once again, it will be "good."

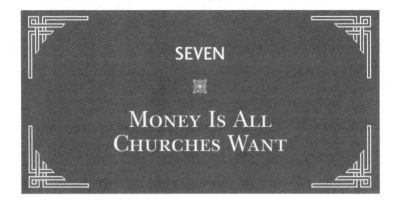

I n an effort to teach respect for religious diversity, a teacher instructed her second-grade students to bring something to class that represented their religion. The students returned with a variety of religious items. A Jewish boy brought a star of David. A Muslim boy brought a prayer rug. A Roman Catholic girl brought a rosary. A Protestant girl brought an offering plate.

It may seem to many people that churches, including Roman Catholic churches, put an undue emphasis on contributions. Fund-raising campaigns are common for everything from property expansion to the purchase of a new sound system.

> "I visited a neighborhood church only a few Sundays and signed the guest book. I should never have signed it. I keep getting financial appeal letters. No way will I go there again."

> "I recently changed churches. My former church hired a professional fund-raising organization to kick off a building

program. The fund-raisers advised members of the Building Committee to canvass the church's constituency for financial pledges. No one from church had visited me before, but Building Committee members came to my house three times to pressure me to pledge. That's when I said, 'Enough is enough.' Now I attend a small church that has a lot of empty seating and no plans to construct a new building."

"My church sends every member a quarterly stewardship statement. It compares what I gave in that quarter to what I gave in the same quarter last year. If my contributions drop below those of the previous year, a letter accompanies the report telling me to increase my contributions. Sometimes, I think my church operates more like a business than a place of worship."

If these remarks seem familiar, you may think money is all churches are interested in, but this conclusion would be an overgeneralization. Most churches are far more interested in ministry than money. They respond to individuals and families in need. They encourage volunteerism. And they donate a high percentage of their income to missionary service.

Churches that take the Bible seriously teach kids, teens, and adults the significance of pursuing deeds of kindness. They explain that Jesus placed a high priority on serving others, just as he did.

When two of Jesus' disciples requested that he appoint them as the top officials in his kingdom, Jesus used the

occasion as an opportunity to teach an important principle.
He called his disciples together and told them:

> "You know that those who are regarded as rulers of the
> Gentiles lord it over them, and their high officials exercise
> authority over them. Not so with you. Instead, whoever
> wants to become great among you must be your servant, and
> whoever wants to be first must be slave of all." (Mark
> 10:42–44)

But Jesus did not demand a lifestyle from his disciples
that he himself did not follow. He always practiced what he
preached. He said, "For even the Son of Man did not come to
be served, but to serve, and to give his life as a ransom for
many" (v. 45).

No Christian can look seriously at Jesus' ministry and self-
sacrificing death without feeling inspired to follow his
example of love. "Love is kind ... it is not self-seeking," Paul
wrote in 1 Corinthians 13:4–5.

Jesus' example of selfless love transformed the attitude of
the two disciples who asked for prestigious positions in the
kingdom. The two were brothers, James and John. Not long
after Jesus rose and ascended to heaven, James laid down his
life for the sake of the gospel (Acts 12:1–2), and John served
the church for decades, becoming known as "the apostle of
love." It was John, at the ripe old age of ninety-plus, who wrote:

> This is how we know what love is: Jesus Christ laid down his
> life for us. And we ought to lay down our lives for our brothers.
> If anyone has material possessions and sees his brother in need

> but has no pity on him, how can the love of God be in him?
> Dear children, let us not love with words or tongue but with
> actions and in truth. (1 John 3:16–18)

Many books could be written to describe the selfless spirit of service displayed by congregations and individual Christians. Perhaps, because I have served quite a few congregations as an interim pastor, I have enjoyed numerous opportunities to recognize Christian love in action.

I have spent long hours with church leaders in prayer and careful deliberation to ascertain the best ways to serve the people who elected them. Their financial accountability was above reproach as the leaders allocated funds for the benefit of needs at home and abroad.

I have known generous Christians who stepped up to the plate on behalf of struggling unemployed heads of households. "Pastor, please see that Rod gets this," a church member instructed as he handed me a hundred-dollar bill. "I'm sure he could use a little help."

Jill, a single mom with a teenage daughter, struggled to make ends meet on a low income. When she found a decent place to rent, her church purchased appliances, gave her a thousand dollars, and moved her furniture and possessions into her new place.

Medical bills soared for a couple whose young daughter suffered from serious birth defects. Their fellow Christians dug into their pockets and contributed a sizable sum of money to help reduce the medical debt.

I have seen church youth groups perform service for the elderly by trimming their shrubs, mowing their lawns, painting their houses, and shoveling their walks.

Writing in the April 28, 2005, issue of the Colorado Springs *Gazette,* Jane Reuter profiled a high-school senior who nearly died when he was a toddler. At age fifteen, he was thrown from a car. Now he volunteers at a local hospital. When asked, "If you had to lose all your material possessions except one, what would you choose to keep and why?" this young man replied, "My Bible. I believe there are only two things that last eternally—and that is the Word of God and the souls of men. One thing I really desire to do is dedicate my life to service in some form or fashion—whether in the medical field, or as a missionary, a military officer—as long as I am serving other people."

In the late 1980s, I served as interim pastor of a small church with a big heart. Although its membership never exceeded forty, the church gave more than fifty thousand dollars annually to missions and held a monthly service at a rescue mission. Most of the church's members were retired and lived on a fixed income. Some subsisted on very little. But no one's need went unmet. If a widow's house needed repairs, volunteers would make them. If someone's car broke down, and the owner couldn't afford to have it fixed, a retired auto mechanic would get it running again.

I am currently the interim pastor of a church with a weekly attendance of less than fifty. The congregation is growing, but none of the members suggest waiting until the congregation doubles before helping the needy. The church houses a food pantry for needy families in the neighborhood, and often helps them financially, as it is able to do so.

Service-oriented congregations dot the American landscape and prove by their charitable actions that they are not self-centered materialists. The term "parachurch organizations" is familiar to most Christians. Although they are not churches, parachurch organizations usually consider themselves an arm of the church and dependent on churches for financial support and workers. Hundreds of parachurch organizations minister to the needs of boys and girls, youth, and adults, often providing significant altruistic services around the world.

Of course, much of their inspiration and motivation is based on the teaching of Scripture their workers receive in their respective churches.

Although I could list numerous parachurch organizations involved in helping needy and helpless people, I will mention the efforts of only a few.

When volatile weather rips through communities with devastating results, Salvation Army workers and Mennonite relief teams are usually on hand to feed and clothe displaced residents and to spearhead the rebuilding efforts.

World Vision, a parachurch organization, has been at the forefront of assisting disaster victims for decades.

Samaritan's Purse, headed by Franklin Graham, maintains relief work around the world, and quickly rushed to the Far East to help victims of the tsunami disaster.

Compassion International ministers to impoverished boys and girls in many foreign countries through its adult sponsors.

International Students arranges homes away from home for foreign students at American universities. Loving Christian families make them feel part of their family circle by including them in such fun-filled activities as picnics, ball games, and relaxing conversation.

Food for the Hungry, another parachurch organization, rushed assistance to tsunami victims and to victims of earthquakes off the coast of Indonesia. According to information on its Web site, Food for the Hungry "helps disadvantaged people in 47 countries through child development programs, agriculture and clean-water projects, health and nutrition programs, education, micro-enterprise loans and emergency relief."

Chuck Colson's Prison Fellowship Ministries carries Christ's love and his message into jail cells and into the hearts of family members whose husbands and dads are behind bars.

Some Christian publishers, like Cook Communications Ministries, represent the church well by distributing Bibles and books worldwide on a nonprofit basis.

Thousands of churches send mission teams to needy communities at home and abroad to demonstrate the love of

Christ in practical ways. They build schools and churches, serve orphanages, and teach skills.

Christian doctors, dentists, educators, and contractors often donate a month or more of their busy schedules to serve where needs exist in third-world countries.

The history of Christianity in Britain and North America reveals how Christians have served at the forefront of efforts to benefit others. Many universities, hospitals, children's homes, and family counseling centers exist because Christians care for others. Again, by teaching Christian values churches have contributed to the caring attitude demonstrated by these good Samaritans.

In fact, churches often tell the story of the Good Samaritan to encourage their members to help the needy. The story originally told by Jesus and recorded in Luke 10:30–35, exposes the wickedness of withholding help from those who suffer.

A self-righteous expert in Jewish law prompted Jesus' telling of the story by asking, "Who is my neighbor?" (v. 29). Jesus had just told him to love God with his whole being and to love his neighbor as himself (v. 27).

According to the story, a traveler was on his way from Jerusalem to Jericho, seventeen miles distant, when robbers pounced on him, stripped his clothes off him, beat him severely, and left him to die. Separately, two prominent religious leaders stumbled onto the victim, but neither of them bothered to get involved. Each one simply continued his journey. However, a Samaritan got involved when he found the victim. He treated his wounds, set him on his donkey, checked him into an inn, and promised to reimburse the innkeeper for any expenses he might incur in restoring him to good health.

Jesus asked the expert in Jewish law, "Which of these three do you think was a neighbor to the man who fell into the hands of robbers?" (v. 36).

The obvious answer applied not only to the expert in Jewish law, but also to everyone exposed to Jesus' story and to churches too. A church may choose to look at the needy but do nothing about the need, or it may follow the example of the Good Samaritan. Churches that choose to take Jesus' story to heart get involved.

Early in the last century, liberal theology transformed the thinking of many churches. They discarded the teaching that human beings can be saved only by divine grace and taught that human beings can earn eternal life by performing good deeds. As a result, they embraced what has been called "the social gospel," and invested time, energy, and money into social programs. However, other churches held tenaciously to a theology of grace. They insisted the "social gospel" eclipsed the true gospel and that their responsibility was to pursue spiritual concerns, not social ones.

In recent years, however, many churches have seen their responsibility as dual: to proclaim the message of salvation by grace and to minister to the needy.

Indeed, the Bible teaches believers to care for the needy, and it indicates that doing so is a significant evidence of genuine faith.

The psalmist Asaph wrote: "Defend the cause of the weak and fatherless; maintain the rights of the poor and oppressed. Rescue the weak and needy" (Ps. 82:3–4).

Solomon, Israel's wise king, commented, "Blessed is he who is kind to the needy" (Prov. 14:21) and observed, "A generous man will himself be blessed, for he shares his food with the poor" (22:9).

But long before Asaph and Solomon lived, before entering the Promised Land, the Israelites received an important injunction from the Lord about charitable treatment of the poor. He commanded them: "When you reap the harvest of your land, do not reap to the very edges of your field or gather the gleanings of your harvest. Do not go over your vineyard a second time or pick up the grapes that have fallen. Leave them for the poor and the alien. I am the Lord your God" (Lev. 19:9–10).

Jesus included proper treatment of the poor in his code of ethics. "If you want to be perfect," he told a rich young man, "go, sell your possessions and give to the poor, and you will have treasure in heaven. Then come, follow me" (Matt. 19:21). This instruction was not a condition of salvation, but a test to determine the rich young man's willingness to value Jesus more highly than wealth.

In Luke 14:13–14, we read these instructions from Jesus:

"But when you give a banquet, invite the poor, the crippled, the lame, the blind, and you will be blessed."

Of course, Jesus could relate well to the poor; he never had a clothes closet, never owned property, never had a place of his own to lay his head; never had a bank account. He even had to borrow a colt to ride into Jerusalem when he formally presented himself as Israel's king. When his crucified body was removed from the cross, it was laid to rest in a donated tomb.

The early church learned to care for the poor and needy and to renounce materialistic ambition. The apostle Paul and his coworkers received instructions from a council of Judean churches to "remember the poor" in their ministry, which Paul reported was "the very thing I was eager to do" (Gal. 2:10).

As Paul preached the gospel, he encouraged the churches he founded to contribute to the relief of the poor in Judea. Furthermore, he followed a wise policy concerning this relief effort. The churches appointed their own trusted representatives to deliver the funds.

The apostle James wrote the epistle that bears his name to exhort believers to show by their good works that their faith is real. He blasted prejudice against the poor and preferential treatment of the rich. In James 2:8–9, 14–17, he wrote:

> If you really keep the royal law found in Scripture, "Love your neighbor as yourself," you are doing right. But if you

show favoritism, you sin and are convicted by the law as
lawbreakers....

What good is it, my brothers, if a man claims to have faith
but has no deeds? Can such faith save him? Suppose a brother
or sister is without clothes and daily food. If one of you says to
him, "Go, I wish you well; keep warm and well fed," but does
nothing about his physical needs, what good is it? In the same
way, faith by itself, if it is not accompanied by action, is dead.

A Drug Enforcement Administration officer pulled me
aside as I was boarding a plane at Chicago O'Hare
International Airport. She gave me a no-nonsense look. "Sir,
where are you going?"

"Toronto."

"What is the purpose of your trip?"

"I am scheduled to preach in a church there."

"Are you an American citizen?"

"Yes."

"Are you carrying more than ten thousand dollars?"

I chuckled. "I'm not that kind of preacher."

Her unchanged facial expression let me know she didn't
appreciate my humor, but she did allow me to board the
plane.

Conceivably, a preacher may have lots of money and
maintain a strong commitment to Christ. He may give away
huge amounts of money to ministries and charitable causes. I
just don't happen to be that kind of preacher. Nor have I ever
been associated with a church having tons of money.

Nevertheless, we should not judge a church by the size of its offerings but by the way it disburses its money. Churches that teach and practice authentic Christian love care more about people's needs than their money.

In his first letter to Timothy, a young pastor, the apostle Paul advised: "Command them [Christians to whom Timothy ministered] to do good, to be rich in good deeds, and to be generous and willing to share" (1 Tim. 6:18). That same advice applies to us today.

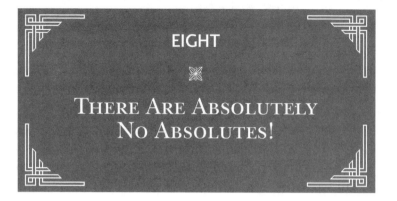

# EIGHT

# THERE ARE ABSOLUTELY NO ABSOLUTES!

You may not know the term "moral relativism," but you have been exposed to this popular philosophy. Moral relativism sees ethical standards, issues of right or wrong, and the defining of morality as subject to personal choice. Each person may decide what is true and what is appropriate.

In a 2002 column from Fox News, analyst Bill O'Reilly asked, "Why is it wrong to be right?" All About GOD Ministries comments: "O'Reilly cites recent Zogby poll findings regarding what is being taught in American universities. Studies indicate 75% of American college professors currently teach that there is no such thing as right and wrong. Rather, they treat the questions of good and evil as relative to 'individual values and cultural diversity.'"

The belief that individual values and cultural diversity are the criteria for deciding moral issues is characteristic of post-modern thought, but how postmodern is it? The Bible associates this philosophy with a segment of Israel's history known as the times of the judges.

The Old Testament book of Judges traces events in Israel's history from about 1380 to 1045 BC. The Israelites had settled into the land of Canaan, often called the Promised Land, but they failed to expel the pagan Canaanites. At times they copied the Canaanites' idolatrous practices despite the Lord's numerous warnings about the judgment this behavior would incur. Sure enough, the Lord punished the Israelites by allowing fierce Canaanite tribes to overpower them and enslave them.

Wincing in bondage, the Israelites eventually repented of the evil that had incurred the Lord's judgment. The Lord responded by raising up judges—deliverers—who liberated the Israelites from their oppressors. But before long the Israelites slipped back into idolatry and other wickedness, touching off another round of oppression.

The book of Judges describes a series of cycles in which Israel went from acceptable moral and spiritual behavior to corrupt behavior to bondage to repentance to deliverance, only to fall again into idolatry and moral corruption.

A stark statement appearing twice in the book of Judges holds the key to understanding why Israel fell into bondage so often. Judges 17:6 and 21:25 report that "everyone did as he saw fit." In other words, moral relativism was the popular philosophy.

Eleven years after the birth of the United States of America, Professor Alexander Tyler warned: "The average age of the world's greatest civilization has been two hundred years.

These nations have progressed through this sequence. From bondage to spiritual faith; from spiritual faith to great courage; from courage to liberty; from liberty to abundance; from abundance to complacency; from complacency to apathy; from apathy to dependency; from dependency back into bondage."

Who can argue that truth is under attack in America? Relativists view those who believe that the Bible embodies absolute truth as divisive throwbacks to an unenlightened era. The Pledge of Allegiance's phrase, "under God," rankles those who want to rid the nation of all public references to divine authority, and any public display of the Ten Commandments sends them scrambling for demolition equipment. After all, if we acknowledge God's authority, we must acknowledge his right to hold us accountable to abide by his moral and spiritual standards.

Fyodor Dostoevsky understood the correlation between belief in God and living by his high moral standards. In his *The Brothers Karamazov,* Dostoevsky reflected, "If God does not exist, everything is permissible."

Although our nation's founding fathers may not have been unanimously Christian and committed to the Bible as absolute truth, collectively they acknowledged God and believed that he had endowed every individual with inalienable rights. The noble principles of life, liberty, and the pursuit of happiness sprang from biblical teaching.

Is America following the cycle Professor Tyler referred to? Having begun so well more than two and a quarter centuries ago, have we slipped perilously close to bondage? Have we become complacent about the moral principles that made our nation free and strong? Have we grown apathetic about truth? Have we become dependent on government to take care of us? Do we expect Washington to do for us what we are unwilling to do for ourselves? We may not be in bondage yet, but it may soon appear on the horizon.

Thankfully, our laws and system of justice still recognize that chaos occurs when "everyone does what he sees fit." Citizens cannot rob a bank and claim to be innocent because they simply did what they saw fit—they needed money, and what better place to find it? A CEO cannot swindle stockholders and get off scot-free because he feels he is above the law. A student cannot expect a passing grade while rejecting absolutes. He may argue that ten times ten equals a hundred only for those who believe it, but if on a test he sees ten times ten equaling fifty-nine, what's the harm? That kind of thinking will get him a failing grade.

We don't have to search long and hard to see moral relativism at work. Rejecting biblical standards of right and wrong, many couples live together outside marriage. Thousands of babies are born to single mothers. Many couples have babies before considering marriage. Thousands of kids live with a father and mother with different last names. Women undergo abortions, thinking, "It's my body. I can do what I want!" Sometimes medical personnel perform abortions on teenage girls without consulting the parents. School officials seem hard-pressed to impose a dress code on students. After all, according to moral relativism, each person can decide what he or she wants to wear. So Jane is free to attend classes in outfits that show more skin than material; and Johnny can wear a skirt if he chooses. Both Jane and Johnny can dye their hair bright orange or red or purple, sport ten earrings on each ear, a ring protruding from the nose, a stud in the nose, and another stud in the tongue. They believe they have the right to do whatever they see fit—whenever and wherever: "It's my life. No one has the right to tell me how to live it!"

The Barna Group, in a report dated November 26, 2001, observed:

> The most startling shift has been in people's views about moral truth. Given the nature of the terrorist attack, one might have expected Americans to become more convinced of the presence of good and evil, and that there are absolute moral principles that exist regardless of cultural realities and personal preferences. However, Barna's research showed exactly the opposite outcome.
>
> Prior to the attacks the most recent inquiry concerning truth views was in January 2000, some 20 months prior to the terrorist activity. At that time, people were asked if they believed that "there are moral truths that are absolute, meaning that those moral truths or principles do not change according to the circumstances" or that "moral truth always depends upon the situation, meaning that a person's moral and ethical decisions

depend upon the circumstances." At the start of 2000, almost four out of ten adults (38%) said that there are absolute moral truths that do not change according to the circumstances. When the same question was asked in the just-completed survey, the result was that just two out of ten adults (22%) claimed to believe in the existence of absolute moral truth.

The people groups least likely to believe in absolute moral truth were Baby Busters (i.e., those 36 and younger—only 13% embrace absolute truth), Catholics (16%) and adults who are not born again Christians (15%). The groups most likely to endorse the existence of absolute moral truths include Baby Boomers (i.e., people 37 to 55 years of age—28% of whom embrace absolute truth), adults who attend non-mainline Protestant churches (32%) and born again individuals (32%).

Interestingly, when people were further queried as to the source of the principles or standards on which they base their moral and ethical decisions, the post-attack survey discovered that only one out of eight adults—just 13%—cited the Bible. The most common sources of guidance regarding moral decisions trusted by Americans are feelings (25%) and the lessons and values they remember from their parents (14%).

Based on these data, we can conclude that acceptance of moral absolutes is declining and that some who subscribe to moral absolute truth do so on the basis of something other than the Bible. But the Bible stands alone as the only infallible source of truth, because it is God's Word. In prayer, Jesus said to the Father, "Your word is truth" (John 17:17).

I would rather trust Jesus to identify truth than to trust either my feelings or the values and lessons I learned from my parents. As good and truthful as my parents were, they were not infallible. On the other hand, Jesus always spoke the truth and lived the truth. The book of Revelation identifies him as "holy and true" (3:7) and "Faithful and True" (19:11). Those who heard him teach commented that he spoke with authority (Matt. 7:29) and that he had the words of eternal life (John 6:68). Even his enemies could find no fault in him. They had to resort to hiring false witnesses to convict him in a kangaroo court (Matt. 26:57–67). Therefore, I believe what Jesus said about the Bible, God's Word: *It is truth.*

An example of moral relativism at work was played out May 1–2, 2005, when about five hundred gay and lesbian protestors representing a movement called Soulforce demonstrated in front of Focus on the Family. The demonstrators objected to Focus's insistence that homosexuality is sinful and that heterosexuality is the only sexual orientation the Bible endorses.

A sign held high by a demonstrator proclaimed, "Love makes a family." Is this true? Does love make a family? The answer depends on what one defines as love and family. Moral relativism would argue that love is whatever an individual decides, and family is whatever that person says it is. The Bible, however, defines love in 1 Corinthians 13 as pure and selfless, whereas in Leviticus 18:22 it identifies homosexuality as an abomination. It defines a basic family as a loving relationship in which "a man will leave his father and mother and be united to his wife, and they will become one flesh" (Gen. 2:24).

The Old Testament presents the Ten Commandments as the standard for moral and spiritual attitudes and actions. The New Testament affirms the moral principles contained in the Ten Commandments and summons Christians to lead a righteous life and aspire to be like Christ. The moral principles contained in the Ten Commandments mold a nation into an orderly society, but moral relativism pushes a nation into confusion and chaos.

Ask yourself what life would be like if your neighbor did what he saw fit. If he thought breaking into your house and stealing was appropriate, would you welcome his perspective? If your boss mistreated you, worked you half to death, withheld a fair salary, and stole from the company, would you respect his right to do what he saw fit to do? According to a 2004 survey of 2,639 employees and managers conducted by staffing firm Randstad North America, 86 percent said they'd prefer to work for a boss who focuses on ethics over profitability.

I suspect that those who believe there are no absolutes change their perspective when they feel victimized. They believe the auto mechanic was wrong to charge for parts and services he didn't provide; the neighbor was wrong to park six clunkers on his front lawn; the checkout clerk was wrong to ring up $1.98 instead of $1.48; the thief was wrong to snatch her purse; the president was wrong to commit the nation to war; the short-order cook was wrong to burn the toast.

Judgments about right and wrong are inevitable. No one can avoid them by saying right and wrong are only in the eye of the beholder. A nation without moral absolutes cannot survive. Authentic Christians put their confidence in the Bible as the source of absolute truth and try to walk in the truth.

# NINE

## IT'S STUPID TO WORSHIP A DEAD MAN

Boulder, Colorado, grabbed media attention in 2004 and again in 2005. Allegations of the use of sex as a lure to recruit football players for the University of Colorado Buffaloes surfaced in 2004. The following year media attention shifted to CU professor Ward Churchill for allegedly calling 9/11 victims Nazis. But in tiny Nederland, only a few miles outside Boulder, another bizarre story slipped into the media.

Nederland was hosting its annual "Frozen Dead Guy" celebration, complete with a parade and fun-filled festivities. The celebration honors Grandpa Bredo Morstoel, whom Nederlanders refer to as "The Frozen Dead Guy."

Grandpa Morstoel died in 1989 in Norway. His body was packed in ice, shipped to Los Angeles, and cryogenically frozen. It seems Grandpa Bredo's grandson, Trygve Bauge, hoped medical science would be able to reverse the cause of death and bring Morstoel back to life. Several years later, Bauge and his mother moved the body from Los Angeles to

Nederland, where it reposes in a shed next to their house. The temperature inside the shed registers a constant minus 109 degrees.

If you think celebrating a "Frozen Dead Guy" ranks high on a scale of weird-and-wacky wonders, undoubtedly you share a majority opinion, but in defense of the good people of Nederland, we can give them some credit. At least they don't worship Grandpa Bredo. No one in his right mind would worship a dead man.

Yet, Christians have been accused of doing so. Those who reject the teaching that Jesus rose from the dead see Christianity as a religion resting on the lid of a casket, whereas believers see it as authentic faith based on an empty tomb. Which group is right?

Before deciding, consider the following implications of a fictitious resurrection.

*The apostle Paul wrote, "If Christ has not been raised, our preaching is useless"* (1 Cor. 15:14). If Jesus did not rise from the dead, every sermon, lecture, and article about life beyond the grave carries as much spiritual clout as whistling "Dixie." No matter how many points this kind of sermon, lecture, or article contains, it is pointless. Theologians, preachers, and inspirational writers should turn their attention to other matters. Indeed, religious liberals who deny the resurrection of Jesus Christ have done so; they have turned their attention to the kind of preaching, lecturing, and writing that strips the supernatural of the "super" and leaves only the "natural."

They focus only on Jesus' life and teachings as precedents for leading a life of high morals and altruism. These liberals credit Jesus with an exemplary life, and exhort us to follow his example. But they do not infuse our lives with the power of his resurrection. They urge us to follow Jesus, but fail to trace his path beyond the grave.

*A fictitious resurrection renders our faith "useless" according to 1 Corinthians 15:14.* Verse 17 adds that our faith is "futile" if Christ did not rise from the grave. Futile faith renders prayer ineffective. A dead man can't hear our prayers. Why bother to ask him to bless our food, guide our steps, protect our loved ones, and stand beside the land we love?

A futile faith mocks every Christian martyr and scoffs at every missionary who has left a comfortable lifestyle and the family circle to share the gospel with people in other lands. If Christ did not rise from the dead, missionary organizations should return every cent donated to them. Every Christian publisher and Christian seminary should close its doors, and every evangelical church should become simply a social agency.

*Further, Paul charged that believers are false witnesses if Christ did not rise from the dead (v. 15).* As you know, false witnesses in a court case can damage either the prosecution or the defense. A false witness may claim that the defendant could not have committed murder on such and such a day because he and the witness were fishing at a remote lake from dawn to dusk that day. Or a false witness may claim to have seen a defendant steal a wad of money from an open cash register of a fast-food restaurant while the counter clerk turned to check on the order. The false witness may simply think the defendant matches the description of the thief, but he sticks to his testimony so tenaciously that the jury believes him and convicts an innocent man. False witnesses may offer their testimony because they have been paid to lie, while some sincerely believe they saw or heard something that incriminates the defendant.

If Christ did not rise from the dead, Christians are as much false witnesses as those who offer false statements in a court of law. Whether they sincerely believe that the resurrection of Jesus is genuine, they are liars if Christ is still dead.

*Paul also told the Corinthians that believers are still in their sins if Christ did not rise from the dead (v. 17).* A dead Savior is no savior at all. Without the resurrection, the message, "I'm not perfect, just forgiven," is ludicrous.

*Another implication of a fictitious resurrection concerns our departed loved ones. If Christ did not rise from the dead, they are lost forever.* Paul opined, "Then those also who have fallen asleep [died] in Christ are lost" (v. 18).

I have officiated at numerous Christian funerals and offered hope to those whose loved ones passed away. I have assured mourners that a deceased believer crossed from temporal life on earth to eternal life in heaven. I have explained that because Jesus rose from the grave, death is not a tragedy but a triumph. It is simply a change of address, a graduation to a far better life, a transition from living by faith in Christ to seeing him face to face.

But without the resurrection of Christ, all the hope I have offered was simply wishful thinking. The departed loved ones entered a state of lostness.

In her late sixties, my mother lay in a hospital room in St. Catharines, Ontario. She could look out the window of her room and see our house on the other side of a small valley. Although she hoped to recover from her illness and return home, she would never see the inside of her home again. She was dying of Hodgkin's disease.

Dad placed a call to Denver, Colorado, to tell me that if I wanted to see Mom alive I would have to come home quickly. I boarded a plane to Toronto, where my younger brother met me and drove me the seventy miles to St. Catharines.

Seeing my mother in an emaciated, weakened condition tore at my heart, but leaving her hospital room a few days later to return to Denver was excruciatingly painful. I said good-bye to my mother, knowing I would not see her again in this life. Had Christ not risen from the grave, any hope of seeing her in the next life would have been groundless.

A couple of weeks later I made another trip to St. Catharines—this time to conduct Mom's funeral service. Because her open casket rested in front of the podium, I saw her body when I addressed family members and guests. Believe me, conducting the funeral drained me emotionally.

Later, at the graveside ceremony, my voice weakened almost to silence as I committed my mother's body to the grave with the closing words, "in certain hope of the coming again of our Lord and Savior, Jesus Christ." I could not have endured the funeral service or the committal service if Jesus had not conquered death.

*Christians are a most miserable class of human beings if Christ's resurrection is fictitious.* Paul wrote in 1 Corinthians 15:19: "If only for this life we have hope in Christ, we are to be pitied more than all men." First-century Christians did not lead a life of comfort as most twenty-first-century Christians do. They did not drive cars to and from work, participate in 401(k) programs, and relax each evening watching TV or playing video games. They didn't play golf on Saturday or take the kids to soccer games. They never had the opportunity to spend a leisurely afternoon at a ball game munching hot dogs, peanuts, nachos, popcorn, and cotton candy while root, root, rooting for the home team. Life was tough. Persecuted because of their faith in Christ, many first-century Christians lost their homes and eventually their lives. They were scourged, beaten, jailed, jeered, and thrown to hungry lions. During the reign of Nero as emperor of Rome (54–68), his servants hoisted Christians onto poles in his garden and set them ablaze. What a pitiable life Christians led if they had sworn allegiance to a dead man! They would have been better off following the pagans' advice: pursue pleasure; eat, drink, and be merry, for tomorrow we die.

Opponents of the resurrection of Jesus Christ construct a barrage of arguments in support of their position, but each one falls under the weight of evidence for his resurrection.

*The swoon theory.* Some argue that Jesus did not die on the cross but merely fainted. They explain that the cool, moist air in his tomb revived him, and he left after regaining his strength.

This explanation demands an incredible amount of faith. It asks us to believe that Jesus revived after being beaten, lacerated by a thorn of crowns, nailed to a cross, fastened there for six hours, and subjected to the thrust of a spear into his side. How could anyone have regained strength after such severe trauma and loss of blood?

Keep in mind, too, that a huge stone blocked the entrance to Jesus' tomb, and military guards watched over it. Even if he had revived, could he have rolled the stone away and slipped past guards who knew they would pay with their lives if they failed to secure Jesus' body in the tomb?

But what we read in John 19:31–34 delivers a knockout blow to the swoon theory. This text informs us that the Jews asked Pilate to hasten Jesus' death and the deaths of the two criminals crucified with him by breaking the victims' legs. Their motive was to avoid having Jesus and the other two hang on the crosses overnight, because the next day was a special Sabbath.

Isn't it ironic that those who clamored for the death of an innocent man would be so concerned about observing a religious holiday so rigidly? But religion has often opposed our Savior. Loyalty to legalistic religion is diametrically opposed to salvation and life offered through Jesus Christ.

What was Pilate's response to the Jews' request? He ordered soldiers to break the legs of the three crucified men.

The soldiers broke the legs of the first criminal. Similarly, they broke the legs of the second criminal. But when they came to Jesus, they saw that he was dead already, and therefore did not break his legs.

*The wrong tomb theory.* According to this theory, Mary Magdalene, another Mary, and a few other women should have stopped and asked directions when they walked toward Jesus' tomb with burial spices in hand. The theory speculates that the women's early morning trip went terribly wrong. In the mist of early dawn, they went to the wrong tomb. Finding an empty tomb, they assumed that Jesus had risen from the dead.

But this theory doesn't hold water. First, the tomb in which Jesus' body had been placed was in a private garden owned by Joseph of Arimathea (Luke 23:50–53). One can understand how the women might find the wrong tomb in a public burial place, but they could not have failed to find the right tomb in a private burial plot. Second, Luke 23:55 mentions that the women had followed Joseph, after he had taken Jesus down from the cross, and had seen the tomb and how Jesus' body had been laid to rest. Third, after finding Jesus' tomb empty, the women reported the event to the eleven disciples and others (Luke 24:9). However, the disciples dismissed their report as nonsense (v. 11). Then Peter and John ran to the tomb to check out the report. John outran Peter, but Peter entered first and found the grave clothes intact without a body (v. 12; John 20:3–7). When John entered and saw the grave clothes, he believed (vv. 8–9). Obviously, they had not run to the wrong tomb. The grave clothes served as Exhibit A that they had reached the right tomb and that Jesus had risen. Finally, if the women and the disciples had gone to the wrong tomb, the religious and political authorities could have easily pointed out the error by leading them and others to the right tomb and pointing to the body.

*The stolen body theory.* The disciples stole Jesus' body and contrived the resurrection story, according to this theory. Sure. And the moon is made of green cheese. Consider how absurd this theory is. The disciples' behavior at the time of Jesus' arrest, during the crucifixion, and after the crucifixion resembled that of frightened rabbits cornered by foxes. They had forsaken Jesus when the temple soldiers arrested him (Matt. 26:47–56). Peter had denied Jesus three times in the courtyard outside the palace where Jesus was undergoing a kangaroo trial (vv. 69–75). Only the disciple John stood by the cross when Jesus was dying (John 19:25–27). After the crucifixion, ten of the disciples huddled together in a room. The doors were locked because they feared the Jews (John 20:19). Cowering disciples would not have engaged the military guards at Jesus' tomb, overpowered them, rolled away the stone, entered the tomb, and stolen Jesus' body. Besides, if they had stolen the body, why would they later preach and teach the resurrection and even lay down their lives for the sake of One they knew was dead?

Following Jesus' resurrection, the Jewish authorities paid the tomb's guards to claim the disciples had stolen the body, but why would they waste the money. Surely, they and the Romans had sufficient resources to recover the body and display it for everyone to see!

The truth is, Jesus rose from the dead!

*The hallucination theory.* This theory purports that the disciples wanted to believe in the resurrection so strongly that the power of autosuggestion took over their thinking. They didn't actually see the risen Christ; they simply hallucinated.

Two strong objections counter the hallucination theory. First, the disciples were slow to believe that Jesus had risen. When the women reported the empty tomb, the disciples rejected their story. Luke 24:11 says, "They did not believe the women, because their words seemed to them like nonsense." Second, when the risen Christ appeared to the disciples in the room with locked doors, he showed them his hands and side as evidence that he was not a spirit but their risen Lord in a resurrected body. Only then, did the disciples rejoice (vv. 36–41).

The disciple Thomas, known as Doubting Thomas, was absent on that occasion. When the believing disciples reported that they had seen the Lord, Thomas insisted,

"Unless I see the nail marks in his hands and put my finger where the nails were, and put my hand into his side, I will not believe it" (John 20:25). A week later, he received the proof he needed. Jesus suddenly appeared again in the secured room. This time Thomas was present. Jesus said to him, "Put your finger here; see my hands. Reach out your hand and put it into my side. Stop doubting and believe" (v. 27).

"My Lord and my God!" Thomas exclaimed (v. 28).

Those who think the disciples hallucinated pose a groundless argument. Thomas would be the first to contradict them.

Other theories have been posited from time to time to explain away or deny the resurrection, but the testimony of the apostles and other eyewitnesses is overwhelmingly in favor of a real, physical, victorious resurrection. The apostle Paul, perhaps the most hateful enemy of Christianity, encountered the risen Christ during a campaign to arrest believers. The event changed his life. He testified to the Corinthians:

> For what I received I passed on to you as of first importance: that Christ died for our sins according to the Scriptures, that he was buried, that he was raised on the third day according to the Scriptures, and that he appeared to Peter, and then to the Twelve. After that, he appeared to more than five hundred of the brothers at the same time, most of whom are still living, though some have fallen asleep. Then he appeared to James, then to all the apostles, and last of all he appeared to me also. (1 Cor. 15:3–8)

Having examined the implications of a fictitious resurrection, we can move to an examination of the implications of a factual resurrection. How does Jesus' resurrection affect those who believe?

*Because Jesus rose from the dead, believers know that God accepted the payment for sin that Jesus made on the cross.* Merchants in bazaars in the Far East may not price their goods. A buyer must put money on the table and add to it until the merchant picks it up. As soon as he lifts the money, the buyer can pick up the item, knowing that the payment was satisfactory. When Jesus died on the cross for our sins, he cried out, "It is finished" (John 19:30). He had offered his life's blood as the payment for our salvation.

One Greek word, *telestai*, gives us our translation, "It is finished." Greeks often wrote this word on a bill of sale to indicate, "Paid in full." Jesus paid for our sins in full so that God could grant us eternal life and forgiveness without our having to add anything to the transaction.

Jesus' resurrection provided proof that God accepted Jesus' payment on our behalf. Romans 4:25 affirms that God raised Jesus up because his death procured for us a cordial relationship with God.

*Because Jesus rose from the dead, believers have a guarantee of eternal life.* Having gathered his disciples together in an upper room just prior to his betrayal, arrest, and crucifixion, Jesus announced his legacy. He promised his followers a home in heaven, answered prayer, the gift of the Holy Spirit, fellowship with the Father and with himself, supernatural peace, and eternal life. He said plainly, "Because I live, you also will live" (John 14:19).

Christians can picture Christ's empty tomb and reflect on the fact that our hope of eternal life intertwines with his resurrection. He conquered death for our sakes, and he grants eternal life to all those who believe in him (11:25).

Death is an unpleasant event, of course, but resurrection waits beyond the grave. When a believer dies, his spirit immediately enters the presence of Christ in heaven. Second Corinthians 5:8 points out that to be "away from the body" is to be "at home with the Lord." Ultimately, though, the spirit and body will be reunited when God raises the body from the dead. First Corinthians 15:50–54 explains that this will happen for believers when Jesus comes for the church. Perishable bodies (dead bodies of departed Christians) will become imperishable (incapable of decomposing), and mortal bodies (living Christians' bodies that are capable of dying) will become immortal (incapable of experiencing death).

So what should we do with a dead body? Should we cremate it or bury it? Some people decry cremation. They think it disrespects the body. But how much respect does a buried body command? After all, it decomposes in the ground. God will resurrect the dead whether their bodies have become ash or dust. He formed the first human body from the dust of the ground, and he can form resurrected bodies from dust or ash.

## It's Stupid to Worship a Dead Man

*Because Jesus rose from the dead, believers have a high priest who is always available.* Forty days after rising from the dead, Jesus ascended to heaven. There, he sat down at the right hand of our heavenly Father—a place of unlimited authority (Heb. 8:1). But the place of authority is also the place of availability. Hebrews 4:15 describes Jesus as One who sympathizes with our weaknesses. Because he lived as a real human being on earth, he knows the fury of the devil's temptations. He can relate to our sorrow, loneliness, weariness, hunger, thirst, pain, and suffering because he experienced sorrow; faced severe temptations; and endured hunger and thirst, loneliness, and pain and suffering beyond description. Yet, he did not sin. He holds the key to victory over life's temptations and trials and grants us victory when we approach him confidently in prayer (v. 16).

Genuine Christians can sing with sincerity and heartfelt gratitude: "What a friend we have in Jesus."

*Because Jesus rose from the dead, believers enjoy moment-by-moment fellowship with him.* He is with us always, wherever we are. We can barely imagine what Jesus' presence meant to the disciples when they accompanied him during his earthly ministry. He graciously talked with them as they followed dusty trails from village to village. He was with them at the end of every long day. He ate with them. And he brought peace to them when the storm clouds burst overhead and a gale-force wind whipped up waves on the Sea of Galilee and threatened to swamp their boat. No wonder the disciples were so forlorn and dismayed when Jesus died. Suddenly, Jesus was no longer with them.

But then he rose, and the disciples' melancholy turned to melody. Songs of joy filled their hearts because Jesus appeared to them, commissioned them to preach his good news throughout the world, and promised them, "Surely I am with you always, to the very end of the age" (Matt. 28:20).

Christians cannot enjoy Jesus' physical presence in this life, but we can rest assured that he is with us. Further, he will never leave us. Hebrews 13:5 conveys his promise to us, "Never will I leave you; never will I forsake you."

If you could choose a famous person to accompany you for a week, whom would you choose? The president of the United States? A charismatic entertainer? A sports celebrity? A billionaire? The presence of any famous person pales in comparison with the presence of Jesus Christ. He is with us always—even to the end.

*Because Jesus rose from the dead, believers anticipate a joyful event.* Before keeping his appointment with death, Jesus assured his disciples that he would come again and take them to their heavenly home (John 14:1–3). Think about it: Jesus, the carpenter of Nazareth, is building a home in heaven for believers, and someday he will catch us away from the earth and transport us to that home. We can scarcely picture the beauty and comfort of our eternal home, but knowing the builder assures us that it will be perfect, flawlessly constructed and furnished. No more home repairs! No more utility bills! No more repainting! No more termite destruction! No more flooding! No more faucet leaks! No more locks and keys! No more homeowners insurance! No more mortgage payments!

Shepherds in the Middle East guide their sheep by walking ahead of them. One by one the sheep follow their shepherd. They may be fearful wading into a stream, but upon seeing their shepherd wade through to the other side, they follow. The Christians' Good Shepherd (John 10:11, 14) has forged "Jordan" and waits in heaven for his followers. Death holds no threat to those who believe that their shepherd is alive forevermore. Because he lives, we too will live!

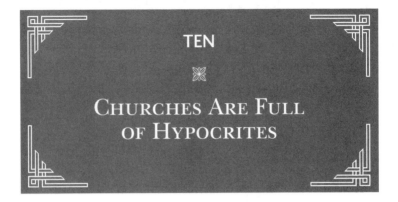

## TEN

# Churches Are Full of Hypocrites

Sixty-year-old Dennis Rader, Wichita's self-proclaimed BTK (bind, torture, and kill) murderer is finally behind bars after slaying ten people dating back to 1974. When he wasn't binding, torturing, and killing innocent people, he worked behind a badge as a compliance officer and served as a Boy Scout leader. He also lived behind the veneer of a respected and active member of a Wichita church. He attended services every Sunday, welcomed visitors, passed out church bulletins, and operated the soundboard. He was a hypocrite.

But are churches *full* of hypocrites?

In recent memory, certain well-known TV evangelists have been exposed for immorality and financial fraud. They duped their viewers and bilked their contributors. They were hypocrites.



But are churches *full* of hypocrites?

Pastors, too, have been caught red-handed in illicit affairs or computer pornography or financial fraud. They were hypocrites.

## Churches Are Full of Hypocrites

But are churches *full* of hypocrites?

Further, we have all known church members who sing like angels in church, but swear like demons out of church. They glad hand fellow worshippers on Sunday, but use slight of hand with clients on Monday. If you shake hands with them any day but Sunday, you had better count all your fingers after the handshake. These untrustworthy church members are hypocrites.

But are churches *full* of hypocrites?

As a young college graduate, I became the pastor of a rural church in 1958. Since then, I have served twenty congregations as a full-time pastor, a part-time pastor, or an interim pastor. I also spent thirty years as a full-time editor at three Christian publishing houses. I think I have seen more than my fair share of hypocrites in the Christian community. Some have cheated; some have manipulated their coworkers or fellow church members for selfish gain; some have abused their spouses or children; some have been immoral; and all of them have lied. Frankly, I detest hypocrisy, even when I am guilty of it myself. And I have been guilty of it. Occasionally, I have counseled anxious individuals not to worry but to trust the Lord, yet I lost sleep because I worried about a health problem. At times, I have led a congregation in the singing of "My Jesus, I Love Thee," knowing all the while that my love for Jesus was not what it should have been. More than once I have exhorted Christians to stand up for Jesus, but sometimes I have backed away from an opportunity to declare my faith in a confrontational setting.

But are churches *full* of hypocrites?

No!

All Christians sin, but most Christians regret doing so. They confess their sins to the Lord and pray for the strength to resist temptation and to do what is right so they can move forward in the Christian life. For every hypocrite who goes to church, there are at least a hundred believers who sincerely try to honor the Lord by leading a righteous lifestyle. Such real-McCoy Christians are the ones who offer a firm hand-shake and a friendly greeting to anyone who shows up at the church's doorstep. They do not discriminate because a person's clothes are shabby or his hair is straggly or his breath is smelly. They welcome the woman in a three-dollar Goodwill outfit as warmly as the woman in an expensive Liz Claiborne outfit. They extend a warm welcome to an eighty-year-old who arrives in a wheelchair, just as they do to an eighteen-year-old who drives up in a Corvette.

We don't have to know many Christians before noticing that most of them are excellent neighbors, take good care of their kids, talk without cussing, help the needy, work hard, pay their bills on time, are worthy of trust, and don't cheat at golf.

~ 122 ~

The Bible doesn't gloss over hypocrisy. It shows that even leaders in Bible times lapsed into hypocrisy and received a firm rebuke from the Lord. It also leaves its readers no doubt that the Lord detests hypocrisy and demands a blameless lifestyle.

Saul, Israel's first king, was guilty of hypocrisy. The Lord told him to destroy a stubborn, evil enemy, the Amalekites. The destruction was to encompass all of the Amalekites and all of their livestock. Although Saul won a decisive victory over the Amalekites, Saul did not do all that the Lord told him to do. He spared the Amalekites' king and the best of their livestock.

The sin of failing to do what the Lord told him to do was bad enough, but Saul added the sin of hypocrisy to it. When the prophet Samuel arrived at the scene of the battle and heard cattle lowing and sheep bleating, he knew Saul had disobeyed the Lord. But Saul greeted him with high-sounding, pious words, "The Lord bless you! I have carried out the Lord's instructions" (1 Sam. 15:13).

*Liar, liar! Royal robe's on fire!*

Saul tried to squirm out of the tangle he had woven by telling Samuel he intended to sacrifice the sheep and cattle to the Lord, but his hypocrisy couldn't hide the truth. He had sinned!

First, Samuel explained that the Lord delights in obedience, not meaningless religious ritual. Then he pronounced the Lord's judgment. "Because you have rejected the word of the Lord, he has rejected you as king" (v. 23).

Hypocrisy exacts a heavy toll.

In the time of the prophet Isaiah, the Israelites practiced religion routinely without genuinely worshiping the Lord.

They kept the religious festivals required by Jewish law; they burned incense, and they spread their hands to heaven in prayer; but they reeked of hypocrisy. Their deeds were evil. They neglected the needs of widows and orphans and engaged in bribery and violence. The Lord responded to such hypocrisy by stating that he would not hear the hypocrites' prayers and was disgusted with their religious observances. He urged the people to repent and start doing what was right (Isa. 1).

The Lord's keen ability to detect hypocrisy hasn't lessened through the centuries. He sees the heart and judges rightly. A hypocrite may assume that his pretense goes undetected, but he is only fooling himself. Eventually, the hypocrisy will come to light and be judged.

A gang of rowdy teenage boys concocted a prank they thought would scare the wits out of a congregation known throughout the community for its emotionally charged worship. One Sunday evening, the gang outfitted one of its members in a devil's costume, complete with horns, a pointed tail, and a pitchfork. After waiting outside the church for the moment when the congregation's worship reached a fever pitch, the gang shoved the "devil" through the church's front doors.

Down the center aisle strode the "devil."

Out the back door and side windows rushed the panicky, screaming church members, including the pastor.

But one severely obese deacon failed to escape. He got wedged between two pews. As he saw the "devil" approach, he pointed his finger at him. "Mr. Devil, stay right where you are. I've been a member of this church for thirty-eight years. But I want you to know I've been on your side the whole time."

Occasionally, a church member appears to be on the Lord's side but is actually on the devil's side, but the phenomenon is rare.

The Lord certainly knows who the hypocrites are, and he will deal appropriately with them.

I suppose it is possible for a church to be full of hypocrites, but this phenomenon, too, is rare.

The first-century church of Laodicea was such a church. Its members were smug and complacent. They went through the meaningless motions of worship, but saw no need for God. The prevailing attitude was, "I am rich; I have acquired wealth and do not need a thing" (Rev. 3:17). The church had even locked Jesus out!

Jesus saw the hypocrisy and warned, "You do not realize that you are wretched, pitiful, poor, blind and naked" (v. 17). He announced, "Here I am! I stand at the door and knock. If anyone hears my voice and opens the door, I will come in and eat with him, and he with me" (v. 20).

Sam and Jared played and walked to school together in an economically depressed neighborhood of a big city. Sam had to drop out of high school and take a dishwashing job to help support his widowed mother and six younger siblings. However, Jared managed to graduate from high school and obtain scholarship money to attend college. Later, he received a large grant from a religious foundation that enabled him to attend seminary in a distant state, where he studied for the ministry. A decade after graduating from seminary, he became the pastor of a prestigious congregation in a highly affluent section of his home city.

One day, while shopping downtown, Pastor Jared bumped into his boyhood friend.

"Sam, it is so good to see you after all these years. What keeps you busy these days?"

"I've been working at the city landfill. I sort piles and piles of trash every day."

The explanation seemed obvious to Pastor Jared. Sam's stained and smelly clothes affirmed Sam's words.

"What have you been up to, Jared?"

"Oh, I trained for the ministry. I am the senior pastor at First Uppity-Up Church in Wealthy Heights."

"Really, what time are your services? I'd like to attend."

Sure enough, Sam attended, and even requested membership. But Jared advised him that he might not feel at home in First Uppity-Up Church. "Why don't you pray about this matter for awhile," he suggested.

It was several weeks later that Sam and Jared met again.

"Hey, Sam," Pastor Jared began. "Have you prayed about joining First Uppity-Up Church?"

Sam looked Jared square in the eyes. "Sure have!"

"What did the Lord tell you?"

Sam answered slowly and deliberately. "The Lord said to me, 'Bless your heart, Sam, do you really expect to get into that church? I have been trying to get in there for fifty years but haven't succeeded yet."

I guess a Laodicean congregation is not exclusively a first-century phenomenon.

Throughout his earthly ministry, Jesus' teachings about truth and genuine faith collided with the lifestyle of the scribes and the Pharisees. These elitists loved to flaunt their religious devotion in order to gain public adoration and applause. But Jesus looked beyond the external show of religion and saw the true condition of the scribes and Pharisees' hearts. What he saw was not good. A person may look great on the outside in his neat, expensive clothes, but X-rays may reveal a serious condition on the inside. Similarly, the scribes and Pharisees appeared to be in top-notch religious form, but their hearts and souls were seriously diseased. Jesus said they were false prophets and warned people to beware of them. He described the scribes and Pharisees as appearing clean on the outside but "full of greed and wickedness" on the inside (Luke 11:39), and as "whitewashed tombs, which look beautiful on the outside but on the inside are full of dead men's bones and everything unclean" (Matt. 23:27). He minced no words when he addressed the scribes and Pharisees. "In the same way, on the outside you appear to people as righteous but on the inside you are full of hypocrisy and wickedness" (v. 28).

These hypocrites appeared to do everything right, but their motives were all wrong. They showed off their religious deeds in order to shore up their own egos. They wanted to be admired by their countrymen. When they gave to the needy, they announced the charitable act with trumpets (6:2). They loved to pray in public to be seen by as many as possible (v. 5). When they observed a religious fast, they disfigured their faces to show they were fasting (v. 16). They gave a tenth of their possessions to God, but they failed to show justice to the needy and genuine love for God (Luke 11:42). They loved prestige and popularity (v. 43).

John the Baptist, who was Jesus' forerunner, also confronted the hypocrisy of the scribes and Pharisees. Seeing them arrive at the Jordan River, where he was baptizing multitudes of repentant Jews, John identified them as a "brood of vipers" and challenged them to "produce fruit in keeping with repentance" (Matt. 3:7–8). Their lives were like a barren fruit tree—all leaves and no fruit—nice to look at but useless.

Even one of Jesus' twelve disciples turned out to be a wily hypocrite. Judas acted as treasurer for Jesus and his disciples, but he loved money far more than ministry. He betrayed Jesus for thirty pieces of silver. Judas was present in the Garden of Gethsemane, where Jesus agonized in prayer and contemplated his imminent crucifixion. So were armed soldiers with whom Judas had made an agreement. He would identify Jesus to them by kissing him. What hypocrisy! A kiss was a customary greeting, a token of goodwill, but Judas employed it as a mark of treason.

You may have read or heard about a church treasurer with his hand in the till or about an unscrupulous Christian entrepreneur who conned retirees into investing their money with him by promising to multiply it almost as miraculously as Jesus multiplied the loaves and fish. Fortunately, such hypocrites are few. I have served twenty congregations as full-time, part-time, or interim pastor, and I have never known a church treasurer to be anything but honest and trustworthy.

Peter, another of Jesus' disciples and a strong leader in the first-century church, urged believers to "rid yourselves of all malice and all deceit, hypocrisy, envy, and slander of every kind" (1 Peter 2:1). He had seen how Judas's hypocrisy had played out, and he had also seen hypocrisy at work in the lives of Ananias and Sapphira, a husband and wife in the early church at Jerusalem.

The fifth chapter of the book of Acts unfolds the sad account of this couple's hypocrisy. The believers in Jerusalem were encountering hard circumstances, especially those who had become believers after coming to the city from distant points to celebrate the Jewish festivals. They had remained in Jerusalem without any way to support themselves. Only the generosity of the resident believers sustained them.

Giving to the relief of the displaced believers was entirely voluntary, but apparently Ananias and Sapphira saw it as a way to look really good in the eyes of the apostles and their fellow believers. They sold a piece of property, and with his wife's full knowledge, Ananias presented some of the money to the apostles. The couple didn't have to give any of the sale money to the relief effort, but Ananias pretended to give it all.

The hypocrisy was short-lived. Somehow the apostle Peter knew that the offering was only a part of the total sale. He accused Ananias of lying to the Holy Spirit. Caught in vice-like fear, Ananias fell down and died.

Sapphira may have been spending a portion of the recent windfall at the Jerusalem Mall when Ananias appeared before Peter. When she arrived three hours later, Peter asked her whether the charitable gift had represented the total amount of the real estate sale. "Yes," she said, "that is the price" (Acts 5:8). Obviously she and her husband had made a pact to deceive the apostles.

"Look!" Peter responded, "The feet of the men who buried your husband are at the door, and they will carry you out also" (v. 9). Immediately, Sapphira expelled her last breath, fell at the feet of Peter, and was taken out and buried beside her husband (v. 10).

Harsh judgment? Yes, but the judgment was not capricious; it was designed to show the infant church that God considered hypocrisy an extremely serious sin.

~*130*~

Apparently, the church got the message. Verse 11 reports: "Great fear seized the whole church and all who heard about these events." Unchecked, hypocrisy would have infested the church and ruined its testimony.

First-century Philippi enjoyed the status of a Roman colony. As such, it served as a center for extending Roman culture in Greece. Citizens of Philippi held Roman citizenship and emulated Roman culture and fashion. However, some residents of Philippi enjoyed an even higher status. As believers in Christ, they were citizens of heaven charged with the privilege and responsibility of modeling the attributes of Christ and spreading his message. It was extremely important, therefore, that these believers lead genuinely Christlike lives.

Therefore, in his letter to the Philippian Christians, Paul mentioned his prayers that the believers there be "pure and blameless" (Phil. 1:10). The word *pure* is an English translation of a Greek word made up of the words for *sun* and *to judge*. The concept of pure lives, then, suggests passing the test of sunlight.

Have you washed a car windshield in the shade, only to find when you moved the car into the sunshine that you had missed a few spots? The "clean" windshield failed the test of sunlight.

The Greek marketplace often included pottery vendors, some of whom were less than honest. They applied wax to cracks and chips in their pottery so that a vase or pot looked good. After purchasing such an item and placing it outside her home, a buyer was soon in for a big disappointment. The sun's rays would quickly melt the wax and reveal the flaws.

To assure prospective buyers that their pottery was flawless and undoctored, honest merchants displayed a sign: *sine cera*, meaning "without wax." Our English word *sincere* comes from *sine cera*. Sincere Christians disdain hypocrisy. Their lives are without wax. What you see is what you get.

My brother-in-law, Bill, entered the United States Secret Service when John F. Kennedy was president, and he retired after a full and exciting career. Most of us associate the Secret Service with the protection of the president and vice president, but Secret Service agents also investigate forgery. They are trained to detect false currency. The longer they study genuine currency, the better they are able to detect counterfeit currency. Similarly, the longer a person observes the lives of genuine Christians, the more quickly he can detect a phony.

Fortunately, genuine Christians abound. If you haven't yet become acquainted with those sincere believers who live in your community, why not get to know some of them now? It just might convince you that hypocrisy isn't rampant in the church after all.

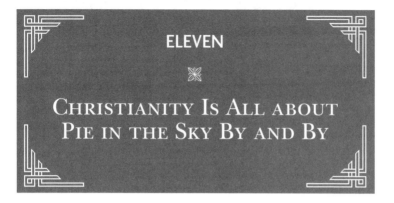

# ELEVEN

※

# CHRISTIANITY IS ALL ABOUT PIE IN THE SKY BY AND BY

S ome restaurants really know their business. Their bakery display case faces you when you enter and leave. Before the host or hostess seats you, you have ample time to feast your eyes on a wide variety of muffins, cookies, and pies. Those mouth-watering desserts are fresh in your thinking when you finish your meal. When you leave, you get another look at the tempting array of desserts. I suppose I should avoid those restaurants. I'm not exactly Slim Jim, but I keep returning to them. Often, I leave with a pie in hand. Key lime is my favorite, but lemon meringue, peanut butter cream, pumpkin, and French apple all run a close second. The truth is, I like any kind of pie except rhubarb. Rhubarb leaves a sour taste in my mouth.

Referring to heaven as "pie in the sky by and by" also leaves a sour taste in my mouth. I think the term gives heaven a bad rap. The eternal home awaiting believers features delights far beyond anything our imagination might create. But Christians who seriously pursue a close relationship with the Lord in this life enjoy current benefits that nothing else can match.

What do most people want out of life? What do you want? If you are like most people, you want to experience loving relationships, peace, a clear conscience, acceptance, and personal fulfillment. Conceivably a person might attain one, two, or three of these goals, but could anyone attain all of them? The Bible answers yes and shows the way.

## LOVING RELATIONSHIPS

John 13:1 reports that "having loved his own [disciples] who were in the world," Jesus "showed them the full extent of his love." John 13 continues with a description of Jesus performing the lowly role of a household slave by washing his disciples' feet. After performing this humble, selfless service, he told the disciples that one of them would betray him, that he would be with them only a little longer, and that they should love one another selflessly. Such love, he explained, would persuade unbelievers that the disciples were Jesus' authentic followers.

Selfless love—the kind of love Jesus showed by washing the disciples' feet and by dying for each of us—doesn't come naturally. "Love yourself!" "Put yourself first!" "Stop thinking about what you need to do for your spouse and children. Think of something for yourself for a change!" These are all familiar sound bites. But when love for oneself eclipses love for others, no one wins. Marriages break apart, kids rebel, charities lack operating cash and volunteers, and neighborhoods become places where strangers peer out of peepholes onto lonely streets.

Christian community offers a difference. Christian homes and churches aren't perfect, but they try to implement the Bible's command to love one another. Christian families strive to live and work together as a loving unit. Congregations try to extend genuine love to their members.

A loving husband considers his wife's interests and needs and places them above his own. He may want to spend Saturday golfing, but Christian love prompts him to give his wife a break. He takes care of the kids so she can shop or simply rest after a long, tiring week. If the family budget permits, he takes his wife and the kids out for a meal occasionally. He shows in many little ways that he loves his wife, and he often shares three important words with her: "I love you."

A loving wife complements her husband. She is his soul mate, best friend, partner, and cheerleader. Her love for him keeps her at his side through every crisis. Gently, but persistently, she helps him become a better man, and often her diplomacy keeps him from saying or doing the wrong thing. If she pursues a career, she places it as a lesser priority than keeping her marriage happy and vibrant.

The institution of marriage is under attack in the twenty-first century. Some couples see it as unnecessary, and therefore they live together without getting married. Feminists may see it as enslaving and a major obstacle to self-fulfillment. Some men may see it as an opportunity to rule as king in a kingdom of two. Nevertheless, God ordained marriage and intended that it should be a permanent loving relationship and the basic structure of an orderly society. When he created Adam, he recognized that man needed a complementary companion. So he formed Eve from one of Adam's ribs and presented her to him. From that first matchmaking operation, the intent of marriage has been to unite two distinct individuals together as "one flesh" (Gen. 2:24).

To be honest, even a Christian marriage can fall apart, but if it happens the fault doesn't lie at the doorstep of the institution of marriage. It lies at the feet of one partner or the other or in some cases at the feet of both. Instead of loving each other selflessly, one or both loved self first and foremost. Perhaps the husband's ego elected him dictator of the domicile. In that self-appointed role he used and abused his wife, allowing her no freedom to think or act on her own. Perhaps the wife decided that her personal pleasure and/or selfish goals were all-important and saw her husband as a roadblock in her way.

According to Romans 5:5, "God has poured out his love into our hearts by the Holy Spirit, whom he has given us." So if Christians fail at marriage, they cannot blame God. An unhappy Christian marriage, separation, or divorce shows that a couple has failed to apply divine love, just as a person's dirty face and hands show that he or she has not used soap and water. The soap and water are not the culprits in the dirty face and hands syndrome. Nor is God's love the culprit in a marriage gone bad. As 1 Corinthians 13:8 affirms, "Love never fails."

Loving family relationships are much more likely when parents and kids are believers. The children honor their parents, and the parents protect the children and guide them lovingly to adulthood.

If you were to ask most Christian parents what is most important to them, they would probably identify God first and their children second. These priorities keep them from sacrificing their children on the altar of career advancement. They spend quality time with their children, instruct them in the Bible, and then coach them to honor God. Attending church as a family is a weekly occurrence, and taking a personal interest in each child's interests and concerns is spontaneous and persistent.

Psychologists often stress the universal need to feel loved. Babies held and cooed over develop better than those who are deprived of loving attention. But what can compare with the love a believer experiences as the object of God's attention? When the apostle John was about ninety years old, he reflected on the incomparable love God showers on all his children. He exclaimed, "How great is the love the Father has lavished on us, that we should be called children of God!" (1 John 3:1).

Knowing that God loves us lavishly isn't pie in the sky by and by; it's a fabulous reality here and now!

## FORGIVENESS

Picture a one-hundred-pound woman carrying a fifty-pound sack of potatoes on her back all the time. Just thinking about it makes me feel that my lumbar disks are ready to pop. What could be worse than being strapped with such a weight? How about having to carry a heavy load of guilt day and night with no relief in sight? Many men and women are doing so, and their consciences are killing them.

Perhaps you lament, "Again and again I have asked God to forgive me, but I don't think he can forgive me; I am so miserable." Have you come to the right conclusion? Can any sin be bigger than God's ability to forgive?

Absolutely not!

God has the power to forgive even the most heinous sins, and he delights to do so. Micah 7:18 attests to this fact:

> Who is a God like you, who pardons sin and forgives the transgression of the remnant of his inheritance? You do not stay angry forever but delight to show mercy.

Examples of God's forgiveness fill many pages of the Bible. He forgave adulterers, thieves, murderers, harlots, pagans, and a host of other men and women who turned to him for pardon and a new lease on life. Examples of his forgiveness also abound today. Christians, forgiven sinners, enjoy spiritual liberation and the power to pursue a life that honors God. Their stories are all different but similar. They received God's forgiveness by trusting in Christ as their

~ 138 ~

Savior. The apostle Paul, a forgiven former hatemonger and accomplice to murder, wrote:

> In him [Christ] we have redemption through his blood, the for-
> giveness of sins, in accordance with the riches of God's grace
> that he lavished on us with all wisdom and understanding.
> (Eph. 1:7–8)

Jesus told a story about a young man who distanced him-self from his father—literally. Fed up with living at home and doing chores, the young man asked his father for an immedi-ate payout of his inheritance. When Dad obliged, the young man left home. He made sure he put plenty of miles between himself and his former life. Jesus said that he set off for "a dis-tant country" (Luke 15:13).

Like a runaway teen with a stack of fifty-dollar bills, this young man wasted his money and himself on the frivolous pleasures to be found in any sin city. Then tragedy struck with a fury.

A severe famine hit the country the young man had adopted. But the country had not adopted him, and when his money was gone, whatever "friends" it had attracted left him in the lurch—homeless, hungry, and lonely. He probably tried panhandling, but that didn't work. After all, famine ruins an economy. Maybe he camped on a street corner, where he held up a sign, "Will Work for Food." Somehow he got a job, but it didn't pan out. The job entailed feeding pigs, but the pay must have been almost zilch, certainly not enough to keep the young man in the manner to which he had been accustomed. With hunger tearing at his ribs, he longed to eat some of the food thrown to the pigs, but no one let him do so.

At the end of his rope but the beginning of his senses, he decided to return home, acknowledge his wrongdoing, and ask his father to accept him as a hired hand.

What a surprise awaited him! When he approached home, he saw Dad running to meet him. Suddenly, Dad's arms encircled him and drew him close. Kisses, not curses, met him.

The repentant son wailed, "Father, I have sinned against heaven and against you. I am no longer worthy to be called your son" (v. 21).

Dad turned to his servants and instructed them to cover his son with "the best robe" and to put "a ring on his finger" and to prepare a sumptuous feast (v. 22). Celebration, not castigation, greeted the returning son who "was dead and is alive again," who "was lost and is found" (v. 24).

Can you picture the joy that swept over the forgiven son's face? Restored to his father, he felt renewed. With nothing to offer his father except a penitent spirit, he received reconciliation, forgiveness, and a special place in the father's heart. Every Christian enjoys forgiveness conferred on him or her by the heavenly Father. We are all prodigals who have confessed our wayward ways and thrown ourselves on the Father's mercy. We deserved punishment, but the Father embraced and pardoned us.

Forgiveness is a treasured possession to be enjoyed now. It is not pie in the sky by and by.

## INNER PEACE

Who doesn't hope for lasting peace in our tumultuous times? Our planet may be a big blue marble, but more often it resembles a red-hot cannon ball that is ready to explode. Terrorists threaten our way of life. Disasters throw communities into upheaval. Crime makes life uncertain. Drug trafficking touches off increasing violence. Schools and courtrooms become shooting galleries. How can anybody experience inner peace?

Millions try to find peace in a bottle, whether a bottle of booze or a bottle of pills. But neither brings genuine peace of mind and heart. Obviously, a physical distress may trigger emotional and mental distress and therefore require medical help that usually involves prescription medicine, but a personal relationship with Christ offers peace for the soul, heart, and mind. A Christian patient on antidepressants experiences the Lord's help as he copes with his illness, and a Christian in excellent emotional and mental health can experience peace even in the most adverse circumstances.

How often have you heard about a peace accord in the Middle East only to hear later that the peace was shattered? The peace Jesus gives his followers contrasts sharply with peace drawn up by fallible political leaders. He said, "My peace I give you. I do not give to you as the world gives. Do not let your hearts be troubled and do not be afraid" (John 14:27).

Christians enjoy peace with God. When they believed in Jesus, they laid down their arms, submitted to God's rule, and entered into peaceful relations with him. In Romans 5:1 the apostle Paul puts it this way: "Therefore, since we have been justified through faith, we have peace with God through our Lord Jesus Christ." One can almost picture Jesus with his arms extended on the cross, taking hold of God with one hand and us with the other and bringing us together into a peaceful relationship.

Occasionally we hear that a preacher has asked a dying person, "Have you made your peace with God?" The question is well intended, but the theology is bad. We cannot make our peace with God, but Jesus made it for us by dying on the cross. In his letter to the Colossians, Paul stated plainly that Jesus made "peace through his blood, shed on the cross" (Col. 1:20). The right question to ask a person, whether dying or not, is "Have you accepted the peace with God that Jesus made for you on the cross?"

But supernatural peace involves more than being at peace with God; it also involves the enjoyment of God's peace. By conforming one's life to the teachings of Scripture and by committing one's circumstances to God in prayer, peace pervades the heart even in the most challenging circumstances. Here are two of the many Scripture passages that teach this truth:

> Great peace have they who love your law, and nothing can make them stumble. (Ps. 119:165)
>
> Do not be anxious about anything, but in everything, by prayer and petition, with thanksgiving, present your requests to God. And the peace of God, which transcends all understanding, will guard your hearts and your minds in Christ Jesus. (Phil. 4:6–7)

Gathering scientific data on hurricanes is essential in helping to protect citizens in hurricane-prone areas, but at least one aspect of this service seems daunting. I can't begin to imagine what it is like to fly into the eye of a hurricane, yet some meteorologists do it. Once in the eye, they find a quiet calm, but getting there can be rough. Often, the Christian encounters hurricane-like forces: medical issues, job uncertainty, global terrorism, a rocky economy, death of a loved one, disastrous loss of property, and many other challenges, but a peaceful calm is within reach. Prayer guides him through each "hurricane" to the "eye."

The writer of the book of Hebrews encouraged his readers to pray their way through life's storms and reach the peace Jesus gives: "Let us then approach the throne of grace with confidence, so that we may receive mercy and find grace to help us in our time of need" (Heb. 4:16).

Sure, heaven is a peaceful place. Once there, Christians will be free from all the pressures and troubles associated with life on earth. However, right now, Christians can experience heavenly peace. There is no pie in the sky by and by in this wonderful quality of life!

## A SENSE OF BELONGING

"Okay, let's choose teams!" Remember these words from your childhood, as you and the neighborhood kids gathered on a playground or corner lot for a game of baseball? Did you get chosen early, or were you the kid standing alone after the captains had picked everyone else? Not a happy feeling to be last, is it? After all, everybody wants to feel accepted.

Apparently dodge ball has come under criticism by some educators who frown on anything that might bruise a student's self-image. They claim it is psychologically harmful to hit a child with a ball and thereby force him out of the game.

It seems everyone wants to be part of a group, to be accepted, to feel a part of some social unit, to feel that he or she belongs.

This need for acceptance and belonging expresses itself in a variety of ways. People of all ages are joiners. They want to belong—to fit in somewhere—so they join such groups as T-ball, Little League baseball, Girl Scouts, 4-H, cheerleaders, high school band, German Club, bowling team, the country club, motorcycle clubs, tour groups, and churches. Often, kids without a sense of belonging seek acceptance by joining a gang, or they hang out with others who feel rejected. They commit crimes and beat up others to fulfill gang initiation rites, or they groom and dress in Gothic fashion. Some women wear red hats and enjoy lunch with other women wearing red hats. Golfers wear hats and shirts that are quite different from those worn by fishermen. After all, they want to be known as golfers! Even when fishing an errant golf ball out of a pond, a golfer is still a golfer. Sports fans wear team jerseys that leave no doubt that they fit in with those who support the Raiders or the Broncos, the Packers or the Bulls, the Nuggets or the Lakers.

We are a nation of joiners, and it feels good to belong to something!

Friends Chris and Rebecca became the proud adoptive parents of a baby boy born July 4, 2004. Appropriately, they named him Sam. My wife and I visited Chris, Rebecca, and little Sam the day he was born. The hospital room could hardly contain the parents' joy, and Sam seemed totally content in Rebecca's arms. On Presidents' Day, 2005, the official adoption ceremony took place in a Colorado Springs courthouse. Again, joy marked a memorable occasion. Even seven-month-old Sam appeared joyful. He smiled widely at his parents and offered baby talk that seemed to express his approval when Mom and Dad vowed to accept and care for him as their legally adopted son. After the ceremony, even the female judge shared in the joy by inviting the family to join her at the bench, where she held Sam, talked to him, and posed for photos. Soon, it was the attorney's time to hold Sam gleefully.

The occasion reminded me of the fact that God adopts believers into his forever family. In Galatians 4:4–5 (NKJV) Paul stated: "But when the fullness of the time had come, God sent forth His Son, born of a woman, born under the

~ 145 ~

law, to redeem those who were under the law, that we might receive the adoption as sons."

Members of God's family enjoy the assurance that their heavenly Father protects them, guides them, cares for them, provides for them, and is always available to listen to their concerns. As a result, Christians journey through life with a profound sense of belonging.

For some, a sense of belonging may be pie in the sky by and by, but for Christians it is a current reality.

## A Meaningful Life

Rick Warren's book, *The Purpose-Driven Life,* didn't become a best seller because of its cover. Its message is what caught readers' interest, especially after news broke that a young woman in Atlanta shared some of its contents with an escaped murderer who had held her hostage in her apartment. In turn he released her. Warren's book communicates the truth that God has an ideal plan for each individual's life. Those who embrace God's plan find significance and fulfillment.

Searching for a meaningful life isn't confined to modern times. In every generation throughout history men and women have searched for it. King Solomon's Old Testament book, Ecclesiastes, identifies paths humans follow as they seek what is truly significant and satisfying. Solomon, like so many others, tried to find significance in pleasure, sex, education, career success, and wealth, but each of these pursuits mocked him. Finally, he turned to God and discovered that a meaningful life is one that honors him. He concluded in Ecclesiastes 12:1: "Remember your Creator in the days of your youth."

If an old person becomes a believer, he has only a brief time to enjoy a truly meaningful life. However a youngster who becomes a believer should be able to anticipate a meaningful life that extends for many years.

Out of curiosity I accessed a Web site that predicts the time of death of each person who keys in brief answers to a few questions (http://www.deathclock.com). The Web site informed me that I do not have very many golf seasons left. But, then, what does a Web site know? None of us can predict how long we have left on earth.

High schoolers in Red Lake, Minnesota, did not know when they left home to attend school the morning of March 21, 2005, that one of their own would kill seven of them and then take his own life. High schoolers usually perceive themselves as immortal or at least destined to live long. But then, life is so uncertain. At any time, any of us may depart quickly for eternity. Life is simply too precious to squander. Proverbs 27:1 reminds us that we must not boast about tomorrow, because we do not know what a day will bring

*Carpe diem,* "seize the day," is not a bad slogan. Wise Christians commit each day to the Lord as an opportunity to serve him. As they do so, they find true significance in the hours and moments. They don't have to wait until they reach heaven; a meaningful life is within reach today.

## THE GIFT OF JOY

Don't let anyone fool you. The Christian life is tough. Becoming a believer doesn't guarantee a life of health and prosperity. Rain falls on Christians' heads just as it does on pagans' heads. Christian homes are not always spared when a tornado thunders and churns violently through town. Cancer strikes Christians as well as non-Christians. A Christian skiing down a mountainside may plow into a tree and break several bones or end up dead. Christians may find themselves unemployed or undernourished. But amazingly even in the worst of times Christians can be in the best of spirits. Why? Because Jesus promised us joy that unfavorable circumstances can't erase. Happiness may depend on having favorable happenstances, but joy depends on having a friend in Jesus.

Instructing his disciples to remain in his love by obeying his commands, Jesus explained, "I have told you this so that my joy may be in you and that your joy may be complete" (John 15:11). He knew his disciples would encounter persecution and deprivation as they represented him in a hostile world. Some would even experience martyrdom for his sake. In spite of severe trials, though, he promised that they would have his joy.

The apostle James counseled Christians to "consider it pure joy ... whenever you face trials of many kinds" (James 1:2). The reason, James explained, is that trials prove the genuineness of faith. Real Christians don't shrivel up and pine away when hard times strike them; they grow up and demonstrate that their faith in Christ is real and that it works. Others may prosper while they have to pinch pennies, but having Jesus is worth far more than all the gold in Fort Knox. So they rejoice. Others may collect roses while they collect bruises, but Jesus, the Rose of Sharon (Song 2:1), is with them always. So they rejoice.

Philippians, a letter in the New Testament, has been called "the Epistle of Joy" because it contains numerous references to joy and rejoicing. Yet, the apostle Paul wrote this letter while under house arrest at Rome. He was undergoing a lengthy court trial and did not know whether he would be set free or executed. The joy of knowing Christ as Savior, Lord, and friend filled his heart and buoyed his soul with optimism and confidence. The outlook may have been bleak, but the uplook was beautiful. Confined to quarters and guarded by elite Roman soldiers, Paul encouraged his friends at Philippi to "rejoice in the Lord always," and added, "I will say it again: Rejoice!" (Phil. 4:4).

Sure, Christians suffer when the car breaks down or a medical diagnosis reveals a serious illness or the boss says "You're fired" or the basement floods, but they understand that their wise and loving heavenly Father allows each trial for their good. They know that he cares and will carry them through the trial and use the experience to refine their character. Therefore, they rejoice.

Christians possess joy as a present reality, not as pie in the sky by and by.

The old Christian woman had died, and her adult children insisted that the mortician place a fork in her right hand. When he asked the reason, they explained. When they were growing up, their mother had always insisted at every meal that they keep their forks after the main course. "The best is still ahead," she would say, referring to the dessert. The fork in their departed mother's hand was their way of expressing the confidence that for Mother the best was still ahead.

The best is still ahead for Christians. Nothing on earth can compare with the beauty and delights of heaven, but in the meantime life on earth includes many benefits that spring from the Lord's gracious hands.

# TWELVE

### THE ONLY HELL IS
### HERE ON EARTH

I sympathize with those who believe that war is hell, and I appreciate the efforts of our military men and women to keep war from breaking out on this side of the Atlantic. But war isn't the hell identified in the Bible.

Poverty and homelessness may seem to be hell to those who shiver under the inadequate cover of cardboard on a winter's night or seek shelter under a bridge or beg for food. But poverty and homelessness are not the hell the Bible describes.

It must be extremely miserable to endure an abusive marriage. I can't imagine the agony a woman experiences at the hands of a husband who beats her or withholds adequate household income from her or in some other villainous manner takes out his frustrations on her and the kids. Such spousal abuse may seem to be hell, but it doesn't fit the Bible's definition of hell.

A job may seem to be hell if the boss is belligerent, the hours are long, the work is almost unbearable, and the pay is negligible. But the Bible doesn't identify a miserable job as hell.

The biblical portrayal of hell defies human comprehension. Hell is real, terrifying, and fiendish. One of Christianity's chief responsibilities is to woo people to heaven and warn them about hell.

Not all Christians believe that hell is a place of unending punishment in literal fire. In recent years some theologians have tried to air-condition hell by finding symbolism in the mention of fire. They believe a God of love would never cause people to suffer the flames of hell. But critics of a literal hell as a place of eternal torment don't seem ready to discard the concept of a literal heaven as a place of eternal bliss. Why is that?

The answer must lie in the fact that sensitive human beings wholeheartedly and quickly embrace what is pleasant and just as wholeheartedly and quickly reject what is unpleasant. Dr. Lewis Sperry Chafer writes:

> Uninstructed minds revolt at the doctrine of eternal perdition and the more sympathetic they are by nature the more they revolt; however, the doctrine does not originate with human reason nor is it influenced by human sympathy. The theologian, here, as always is appointed to discover and defend that which God has revealed. That asserted in the Bible is consonant with the higher divine reason. The root difficulty of all human speculation is the fact that man knows the meaning of neither sin nor of holiness, and these two factors are about all that is

involved in this discussion. The answer of infinite holiness to sin is perdition and retribution.... When the creature knows the evil character of sin as God knows it and the perfection of holiness which sin outrages, then he may sit in judgment on the question of whether eternal retribution of men and angels is consonant with the character of God. It is thus clear that no creature is in a position to deny the righteousness of eternal perdition or to remonstrate against the Creator because of what He does. (*Systematic Theology*, Vol. IV, Dallas Seminary Press, 1957, pp. 427–28)

You may be surprised to learn that Jesus made more comments about hell than he did about heaven, and not once did he suggest that his listeners should apply a symbolic meaning to what he taught.

Jesus warned, "Do not be afraid of those who kill the body but cannot kill the soul. Rather, be afraid of the One who can destroy both soul and body in hell" (Matt. 10:28). If we reflect for even a moment or two on these words, we discover a few interesting truths.

*First, we discover that Jesus believed in a literal place called hell.*

*Second, we learn that the soul lives on after the body dies.* A person may kill the body but not the soul.

*Third, we discover that even the body will be in hell.* Jesus promised to raise the bodies of all the unbelieving dead for judgment:

> "I tell you the truth, a time is coming and has now come when the dead will hear the voice of the Son of God and those who

hear will live. For as the Father has life in himself, so he has granted the Son to have life in himself. And he has given him authority to judge because he is the Son of Man.

"Do not be amazed at this, for a time is coming when all who are in their graves will hear his voice and come out— those who have done good will rise to live, and those who have done evil will rise to be condemned." (John 5:25–29)

Although believers and unbelievers alike will experience resurrection, their resurrections will occur at different times. The resurrection of Christian believers will occur at the rapture (1 Cor. 15:51–52; 1 Thess. 4:13–17), and the resurrection of believers who died in Old Testament times will take place when Jesus inaugurates his kingdom on earth (Dan. 12:1–3). At the end of Jesus' kingdom rule, the resurrection of unbelievers will occur. Revelation 20:11–13 pencils in this appointment and links it with the great white throne judgment. At that time God will consign all unbelievers to eternal hell (vv. 14–15).

The apostle John described this fateful event:

Then I saw a great white throne and him who was seated on it. Earth and sky fled from his presence, and there was no place for them. And I saw the dead, great and small, standing before the throne, and books were opened. Another book was opened, which is the book of life. The dead were judged according to what they had done as recorded in the books. The sea gave up the dead that were in it, and death and Hades gave up the dead that were in them, and each person was judged

> according to what he had done. Then death and Hades were
> thrown into the lake of fire. The lake of fire is the second death.
> (Rev. 20:11–14)

The lake of fire mentioned in Revelation 20:14 is the "hell" Jesus mentioned in Matthew 10:28, warning his listeners to fear the One who is able to destroy both soul and body in hell. The Greek word translated "hell" in Matthew 10:28 is *geenna (Gehenna),* and it occurs frequently in the Gospels. Originally *geenna* (Hebrew: *ge hinnom*) identified a ravine south of Jerusalem. Human sacrifices by fire in honor of the pagan god Molech were made there during the reigns of King Ahaz and King Manasseh. Later, the place became a city dump where refuse was burned. The name *ge hinnom* (Gehenna) naturally became a figure for hell.

But what is hades? Revelation 20:13 depicts hades as giving up its dead for sentencing to the lake of fire.

Hades generally represents the unseen world, but often it identifies specifically the place of punishment between death and the great white throne judgment. One of Jesus' stories focuses on hades and draws back the curtain of death to give us a glimpse of that horrific place.

In Luke 16:19–31, Jesus said that a rich man and a beggar named Lazarus lived contrasting lives. Apparently the rich man showed no interest in God. Surrounded by luxury, wrapped in expensive garments, and accustomed to eating haute cuisine, he must have felt that he didn't need God (v. 19). Lazarus, the beggar, sat at the rich man's gate and longed for the scraps that fell from the rich man's table. Dogs licked the sores that covered his body (vv. 20–21). However, it seems that the beggar believed in God. Eventually, both men died. Angels carried the beggar to a place of paradise, where he enjoyed the company of Abraham, the father of Israel. The rich man landed in hell (hades) (vv. 22–23).

The rich man experienced suffering. Verse 23 reports that he was in torment. He was conscious. He looked, he spoke, and he experienced feelings. He longed for relief, but found none. He mentioned that he was "in agony in this fire" (v. 24). Further, he wanted someone to warn his five surviving brothers about hell, because he did not want them to share the same fate (vv. 27–28). His request was denied on the grounds that the Old Testament Scriptures offered sufficient warning. If they would not heed the Scriptures, they would not heed the warnings given by a messenger who returned from the dead (vv. 29–31).

In summary, hell is a real place with real occupants who experience conscious suffering and a deep concern for the salvation of their loved ones. Further, the Scriptures offer sufficient warning about hell.

"If someone would return from the dead and tell me how to avoid hell, I would believe." This pledge ignores the fact that Jesus returned from the dead and commissioned his followers to proclaim the good news of salvation worldwide (Matt. 28:18–20). He died to make it possible for human beings to escape hell, and he lives to save all those who believe in him. Hebrews 7:24–25 explains: "Jesus lives forever.... Therefore he is able to save completely those who come to God through him."

Of all the religions of the world, only Christianity offers a Savior who rose from the dead. Each of the others may commemorate its founder's birth and death, but none can point to an empty tomb.

Will God allow a second chance for those who die and go to hell? I was quite surprised in college that some professors allowed failing students to take makeup tests, but I can assure you that God does not offer the dead a second chance to be saved. Hebrews 9:27 states categorically, "Man is destined to die once, and after that to face judgment."

To be sure, people in Christianized nations have many opportunities to believe. At almost any time of day or night a person can hear the message of Christ broadcast on television or radio. Christian books run in the millions. They are offered at Christian bookstores, big-box stores, and secular bookstores, and they often show up at neighborhood garage sales. Newspapers and magazines occasionally feature stories of well-known figures whose lives turned around dramatically when they believed in Christ as Savior. Churches that proclaim the message of everlasting life through faith in Christ are located in villages, cities, country towns, and along rural roads. In addition, committed Christians share their stories of personal salvation. It is not uncommon to hear about Christ from a college professor, a barber, an auto mechanic, a plumber, a lawyer, a surgeon, an accountant, or someone in another walk of life.

Most people have no excuse for rejecting Christ.

And unbelief is the only sin that seals a person's eternal destiny in hell. God prepared the lake of fire "for the devil and his angels" (Matt. 25:41). God certainly doesn't want anyone to perish, but all those who reject his Son will perish. John 3:16 reveals the extent of God's love and desire to save us. He gave his only begotten Son for us and invites us to believe in his Son and receive everlasting life.

Indeed, hell is a place of unbearable and unending misery. The book of Revelation describes it as a "bottomless pit" (9:2 NKJV), as a place where there is "no rest day or night" (14:11), and as "the fiery lake of burning sulfur" (21:8). The apostle Jude wrote that hell is a place of "blackest darkness" (v. 13). Jesus called it a place of eternal, unquenchable fire (Matt. 25:41; Mark 9:44, 46 NKJV), a "fiery furnace, where there will be weeping and gnashing of teeth" (Matt. 13:42). But, as dreadful as the physical suffering in hell is, the separation from God must be much more dreadful. Jesus' story of the rich man and Lazarus reveals that a great chasm separated the rich man from Lazarus—from hades and paradise—and prevented movement from one place to the other. Throughout eternity, the doomed will find themselves irreversibly separated from God and heaven. Nothing can be worse than eternal condemnation far from God and the beauty and pleasures of heaven.

## THE ONLY HELL IS HERE ON EARTH

In April 2005, rogue waves, some as high as seventy feet, crashed over the bow of a cruise ship. Ocean water cascaded down hallways and poured into cabins. Many passengers expected to die, but no one lost his life. Later, each passenger who was interviewed by the media related the horror of their brush with death. When asked whether they would take another cruise, each answered with one forceful word: "Never!"

If someone asked, "Do you want to go to hell?" how would you respond? Knowing that hell is a place of endless suffering and anguish, the only reasonable answer is, "Never!"

Additional copies of *All Good People Go to Heaven and
Other Religious Lore*
are available wherever good books are sold.

If you have enjoyed this book, or if it has had
an impact on your life,
we would like to hear from you.

Please contact us at:

HONOR BOOKS
Cook Communications Ministries, Dept. 201
4050 Lee Vance View
Colorado Springs, CO 80918

Or visit our Web site:
www.cookministries.com

HONOR **HB** BOOKS
*Inspiration and Motivation for the Seasons of Life*